THE WAY OF
THE CRAFTSMAN

W. Kirk MacNulty was born in California in 1932. He studied at Standford University and the University of Tennessee, and has followed military and business careers. His involvement in freemansonry spans more than 25 years. He lives in London.

W. KIRK MACNULTY

THE WAY OF
THE CRAFTSMAN

A SEARCH FOR THE SPIRITUAL
ESSENCE OF CRAFT FREEMASONRY

ARKANA

LONDON AND NEW YORK

First published in 1988 by ARKANA Paperbacks
Routledge
11 New Fetter Lane, London EC4P 4EE

Published in the USA by ARKANA
Routledge
a division of Routledge, Chapman and Hall, Inc.
29 West 35th Street, New York, NY 10001

Set in Sabon 10/11 point
by Witwell Ltd, Southport
and printed in Great Britain
by The Guernsey Press Co. Ltd,
Guernsey, Channel Islands

Library of Congress Cataloging in Publication Data
MacNulty, W. Kirk.
The way of the Craftsman: a search for the spiritual essense
of Craft Freemasonry/W. Kirk MacNulty.
p. cm.
Includes index.
1. Freemasonry – Symbolism. I. Title.
HS425.M32 1988
366' . 1 – dc 19 87-37107

British Library CIP Data also available
ISBN 1–85063–108–5 (p)

For my teachers
J.S.G.
W.A.R.
W.D.K.

Contents

Preface

This book is an interpretation of the symbolic structure of Craft Freemasonry. During some twenty-five years I have undertaken to apply the principles of the Craft to my own life and to observe them operating in the lives of others. In the pages that follow I have set out the understanding which I have derived from that undertaking. Clearly, this work represents a personal view based on individual experience and the material is in no way 'the authorised', or 'the one, true' interpretation. It is important to recognise this because throughout the text I have used such terms as 'the Craft represents...', 'the Craft's position is...', or 'according to the Craft's symbolism...', and the reader must understand that I have written in this way only to avoid the clumsy constructions which identifying each statement as my own opinion would have required.

While this does not purport to be a scholarly book, I have tried to present the material in a manner which is consistent with the contemporary academic understanding of the historical period within which the Craft evolved. In a similar way, I have tried to relate the material to the theories of contemporary psychology where that is appropriate. In that respect I am indebted to Ms Amelie Noack for her critical analysis of my application of psychological principles.

Although the work is an original interpretation of Craft symbolism, it is in no sense of the word an exposé. No detail of Masonic symbol is revealed here which has not been published previously and the seeker after sensational material must look elsewhere. On the other hand, I would hope the non-Masonic reader might find that this book gives him the 'favourable opinion pre-conceived of the Order' which, in my opinion, the Craft deserves to enjoy and which is a prerequisite for membership. For the Mason, this book may offer a different perspective of the Craft.

It is a commonplace among Masons that the three evenings spent as a candidate for the three degrees are among the most profoundly moving experiences in one's life. The rituals are constructed to evoke such a response in human beings and they are as effective today as they ever were. For most Masons the intensity of their experience as candidates fades and they settle into the practice of the Craft as a pleasant social institution with a strong ethical and moral flavour. To this majority of Masons the contents of this book will seem strange, unfamiliar and perhaps a little disturbing.

Now and then, however, there is one for whom the experience as a candidate remains bright and alive. It nags at him, so to speak, and demands that he look more deeply into the symbolic structure of the ritual. As he does so he finds that the Craft becomes richer and more relevant until, at last, it provides direction in every aspect of his life. It becomes a guide which will lead him on a long and arduous journey; a journey, which, if he chooses to pursue it, will not end until he has reached the source of his being. This book is written for him.

Such a man has entered the Way of the Craftsman.

London
Spring 1988

CHAPTER 1
Background

1 THE MYSTERIES

There is a body of knowledge which is the property of the Race of Man. It is old – as old as the race itself.

It is, and has always been, available in every culture and in every historical period. In each culture information about this lore is presented in a different idiom, the idiom appropriate to the people of that place and time. Beneath the idiom, the content of the information presented is identical.

This body of knowledge is universally and freely available to anyone who is willing to look. In some periods when the prevailing general attitudes are hostile, the information is carefully concealed and one must look hard to find it. At other, more tolerant times the information is openly available to the casual observer. In general, a relatively small number of people choose to pursue this knowledge because to do so requires one to accept individual responsibility for one's self. That, for many people, is an impassable hurdle; and so the body of knowledge continues to exist, always available, just below the general awareness of society.

The subject of this body of knowledge, which in the Ancient World was called 'The Mysteries' and today is generally called simply 'The Work', is the nature of man. Although the Mysteries are Theistic, in that they premise the existence of some Supreme Being and espouse the view that a consideration of the Deity is properly included in all human endeavours, they differ from religion, first, in that the material relates to man and to this life; and second, in that they do not offer salvation in a life hereafter. As a consequence of these characteristics the Mystery systems are usually found in some form of association with established religious bodies. The area of human activity investigated by the Mysteries lies beyond the threshold of consciousness (as distinct from phenomena beyond the threshold of perception, which are within the domain of physical science) and thus includes, but is not limited to, the unconscious as it has been defined by contemporary psychology.

In the last half of the twentieth century there has been a substantial demand in the western industrial societies for teachings of this sort. Many westerners have turned to eastern contemplative practices because the materialistic west does not appear to offer much in the way of a tradition of interior development. In many respects this is desirable because it fosters a much needed understanding between east and west, and it certainly indicates a trend in western society toward a somewhat less materialistic view of the world. In other ways, however, this western use of the eastern traditions can lead to difficulties. The specific formulations of the Mysteries are almost always stated in the idiom of the culture in which they originate. A cultural gap between teaching and candidate can often produce spectacular misunderstandings and this is particularly true when the subject is as abstract as the functioning of human consciousness. For this reason there are real advantages in following a tradition which derives from one's own culture, if that is at all possible. The thesis of this book is that the Masonic Order embodies such a western Mystery tradition. In the chapters that follow we will examine Freemasonry from that point of view. However, before we can undertake that analysis we will need some frame of reference within which to consider the material. To obtain that frame of reference we will look first at the historical back-ground to Freemasonry, at some of the concepts on which it is based, and at contemporary psychology's view of man.

2 HISTORICAL CONSIDERATIONS

Our purpose in considering historical material is to establish some link between the Craft as it exists today and the ancient disciplines which we have called 'The Mysteries'. Writers who try to establish that link usually ascribe some historical authority to the legends which are to be found within the Craft's ritual. They use that 'evidence' to show that the Craft itself originated in ancient times. While valid in its own terms, such an approach does little to convince those who give serious thought to the subject. Moreover, claims of that sort contradict the real evidence that is available which suggests that the Craft is of relatively recent origin – probably not older than five hundred years, at most. Our approach to making a connection between the Craft and its ancient predecessors will be to look at the history of thought. We will not attempt a thorough study of the subject (indeed, contemporary scholars do not yet have a complete understanding of the period which is of interest to us); we will try only to describe the intellectual climate within which the Craft evolved as a means of determining the context within which to interpret its symbolism.

Freemasonry itself came into existence in its present general form in 1717 when four Lodges which had been meeting in London 'since time immemorial' joined to form the Grand Lodge of England, the first such body to exist anywhere in the world. There is very little accurate information about the Craft prior to that time. We know of a few isolated incidents – for example, that Elias Ashmole was made a Mason in 1646 and Sir Robert Moray in 1641 – but very few facts are available; and in his recently published History of English Freemasonry John Hamill lists only nineteen verifiable events prior to the funding of the Grand Lodge (John Hamill, *The Craft*, Crucible, 1986). After considering what evidence is available, most serious historians (Masons and non-masons alike) who have examined the subject consider that the Order evolved in the late 1500s or early 1600s that is, during the English Renaissance. It is to the history of the Renaissance and of Renaissance thought that we will give our attention.

The Renaissance is a difficult period to study. If one stands well back and views it as a whole (say from the Great Plague in 1347 to the founding of the Royal Society in 1660) one can see it as a period of the most profound social change. Western civilisation entered the Renaissance as an otherworldly society with a religious orientation and emerged from it as a pragmatic society with a materialistic orientation. The mechanism of this profound change is still not completely understood.

Until relatively recently historians have recognised two principal schools of thought as being characteristic of the period: Scholasticism, which was of medieval origin and formed the basis of the rigorous views of the Catholic Church; and Humanism, which was of Renaissance origin and was substantially more liberal in its outlook. The interaction of these two ways of thinking is conventionally considered to have been played out against the background of the contest for power between the Papacy (and the Church in general) and the Holy Roman Emperor (and the secular authorities in general). This struggle had been the major social ideological issue of the Middle Ages and was to continue well into the sixteenth century.

We can say, somewhat arbitrarily, that Humanism started in the middle of the fourteenth century with a resurgence of interest in the study of the Classical world. The Humanists developed a perspective on the Classics which had not been possible within the strictly defined limits of Scholastic thought. The Humanist view focused on man (who was considered to be unique because of his ability to learn), on human values, and on human superiority over nature. In particular the Humanists valued the free will of human beings, and their ideas came to be more and more man-centred, to consider 'man as the measure of all things'. All the richness and creativity of Renaissance art and literature has been until recently generally considered to have been the product of this new freedom of man-centred thought. It goes without saying that such a way of thinking must have come in conflict with the Roman Church. In fact, Humanist thought developed along two lines. One was the reform of the Papacy, which envisaged significant changes in doctrine as well as the correcting of such well known abuses as the selling of indulgences and benefices. This branch of Humanism emerged as the Reformation and reached its culmination in 1517 when it resulted in the formation of the Protestant churches. These independent churches had a powerful (if dangerous) appeal to many monarchs who were still caught up in their power struggle with the Papacy. Many embraced one of the Protestant faiths and imposed it on their subjects for secular reasons. The other line of Humanist thought devoted its attention to secular matters and developed the techniques of critical analysis and experimental investigation. Modern critical scholarship and the scientific method are, in part, descended from this way of thinking.

The position of Catholic Scholasticism was much more complex. While Humanism was new with the Renaissance, the Church was an established institution. It had filled the vacuum left by the demise of the Roman Empire, and had been the only agency to hold European society together during the Dark Ages. It had acquired substantial secular power and materialistic interests in the process; and its scholastic philosophy supported these as well as the religious doctrines of Latin Christendom. As we shall see, there was within the Church substantial recognition of the need for reform, both in terms of correcting the corrupt practices and revitalising the doctrines. It would appear that the inertia which accompanied the Church's materialistic interests prevented the effective interior reform which might have made the Protestant Reformation unnecessary. When internal reform did come to the Catholic Church it was in response to the open rebellion of the Protestant churches, and it took the form of the Counter-Reformation.

The Counter-Reformation had three main objectives: the long overdue internal reform: the re-establishment of Papal authority throughout Europe; and the eradication of the Protestant heresy. The internal reform was apparently very real. The doctrines were restated at the Council of Trent between 1545 and 1573, and several Orders, such as the Ursulines, Capuchins and the Jesuits were formed. The latter Order, in particular, was effective in teaching the doctrines and enforcing the prohibition of abuses which emerged from the Council. This internal reform did much to slow the growth of the Protestant churches and to re-establish the Catholic Church's spiritual orientation. The re-establishment of the Papal authority over the Protestant states of Europe took the form of the military operation we know as the Thirty Years' War. It was undertaken by the Catholic League under the leadership of the Habsburg rulers of Spain and Austria. It certainly failed in its objective to re-convert Protestant Europe to Catholicism. It succeeded only in exhausting the participants and hardening the positions of both sides. The eradication of heresy was the task of the Papal Inquisition. That institution was reconstituted in 1542 and (together with the inciting of witch-crazes) during the sixteenth and seventeenth centuries it effectively eliminated all traces of Protestants from Italy, Spain and France.

In this brief sketch of the conventional and generally familiar view of the Renaissance one sees the Catholic and Protestant churches, together with the princes who supported them, expending their energies in religious conflicts and terminating the intellectual and artistic Renaissance in the process. Meanwhile, the more secularly inclined Humanist bides his time, adapts to the changing situation, and emerges in the relative stability of the mid-to-late seventeenth century to found such institutions as the Royal Society, establish the physical sciences and make way for the Age of Reason.

Within the last thirty years it has become increasingly clear that this generally accepted view of the Renaissance and its philosophies is incomplete. Contemporary scholarship has shown that, in addition to the Catholic and Humanist viewpoints, there was a third body of thought which had a profound influence on the period. (This work has centred on the researches conducted at the Warburg Institute at the University of London and particularly on the work of Frances A. Yates. Most of the material which follows is derived from her work. See especially her books *The Occult Philosophy in the Elizabethan Age* (Ark edition, 1983), *The Art of Memory* (Ark edition, 1984), *The*

Rosicrucian Enlightenment (Ark edition, 1983), and *Giordano Bruno and the Hermetic Tradition* (Routledge & Kegan Paul, 1964). This third body of thought was based on a combination of Neoplatonic and Hebrew mystical philosophy which was very old (or thought to be very old) and which emerged from the Humanist rediscovery of the Classical world. It is important for our consideration because it is beginning to appear that this third body of thought may have been a major factor in the cultural development of the Renaissance. It was certainly central to much of the intellectual life of the period, and it came into prominence because of the capture of two cities.

In 1453 the city of Constantinople was captured by the Turks. As a result of this loss to Christendom a large number of manuscripts which had been salvaged from the libraries of that city found their way via the Mediterranean trade routes to the prosperous mercantile centres of Italy and in particular to the culturally brilliant court of Cosimo di Medici whose family ruled Florence more or less openly from 1434. These manuscripts included the writings of Plato and a number of neo-platonic works from the second and third centuries AD. These latter documents may have originated in the neo-platonic schools at Alexandria where their authors could have acquired the influence of Hellenised Judaism which some of the texts exhibit. They are, in any case, written in an apparently Egyptian form, and comprise the main body of a literature of mystical experience which is currently called the *Hermetica*. The cosmos is presented in these works in an astrological idiom, which was easily accessible to the fifteenth-century European Christian; and the writings relate to the application of divine laws, expressed in astrological terms, to the individual's life and experience.

Marcilio Ficino, the Italian physician, priest and scholar, who translated the Hermetic documents for his Medici employers, was convinced that these writings were Greek translations of the work of Hermes Trismegistus, whom he conceived to be an Egyptian contemporary of Moses. To this devout Renaissance scholar who was steeped in the doctrine that what was old was holy because it was closer to man in his Edenic state, such a document must have had a sanctity almost on a par with the scripture itself. As his translations revealed concepts which appear in both Platonic philosophy and Christian doctrine, Ficino (who had no knowledge of the documents' real origin) became convinced that he was working with the basic material which had been transmitted to Plato via Pythagoras and was actually a pagan prophecy which foretold Christianity. This interpretation was convenient because it made the study and use of Hermetic material acceptable in the eyes of the Church. The antiquity of the *Hermetica*, based on Ficino's erroneous beliefs, continued to be accepted until early in the seventeenth century.

In 1492 the city of Granada was captured by Ferdinand and Isabella. It was the last of the Moorish strongholds in Spain and its fall opened the way for the implementation of Torquemada's policy of 'an all Christian Spain', a policy which resulted in the explusion (or enforced conversion) of Spanish Jews and Muslims. The expulsions marked the end of several centuries of remarkable philosophical and cultural development. Until the latter part of the fifteenth century Christian, Muslim and Jew had lived in Spain in close proximity and in relative peace and harmony. In cities such as Toledo and Cordoba many ideas had been exchanged between Kabbalists, Sufis and Christian mystics, ideas which had a profound effect on the development of each region. This situation of religious tolerance and mutual respect deteriorated gradually with the progress of the Christian reconquest of Spain. Even before the expulsion in 1492 life had been increasingly difficult for Spanish Jews, and there was a steady trickle of emigration to more hospitable countries – including Italy. There must have been Kabbalists among those early emigrants because as early as 1486 Pico della Mirandola, another of the neo-platonists in the Medici circle, made his famous offer to reconcile nine hundred theses which he had derived from Christian, Hebrew, Muslim and pagan sources. Among these were seventy-two Kabbalistic propositions which, in Pico's view, showed Hebrew support for the Christian religion. In fact, Pico practised a form of fifteenth-century Spanish Kabbalah which he had Christianised by proving (at least to his own satisfaction) with Kabbalistic argument that Jesus was the Messiah. Like his Hermeticist colleague, Ficino, Pico found in Kabbalah a confirmation of the tenets of Christianity which made its practice acceptable to the Church.

It may seem strange that the Church, which was to re-establish the Inquisition in 1542 for the very purpose of combating these 'heresies', should be willing to permit and even encourage their practice around 1500. To understand this, one must recognise a point which was (and still is) fundamental to Christian doctrine. In the Christian view the Old Testament is considered to be a prophecy of the New. If we examine the Christian year we find that each festival celebrates not only an event in the life of Christ, but also the event in the Old Testament which is thought to foretell it. From this point of view additional prophetic material from Jewish and pagan sources was to be expected, and might actually be seen to strengthen the position of Christianity. Moreover, such non-Christian material could be (and was) used as powerful argument and justification for the conversion of Jews and others to Christianity; an activity to which the Church gave much attention. One gets the impression that the re-establishment of the Inquisition in 1542 was as much a reaction to the secular situation, which had got out of hand with the establishment Protestant states, as it was to the non-Christian doctrines themselves. In fact, as the *Hermetica* became more generally available and Kabbalistic documents flooded into Italy after 1492, many prominent churchmen considered the Hermetic/Kabbalistic tradition as an appropriate basis for the internal reform of the Church, and produced a widely distributed literature on the subject.

Francesco Giorgi was such a man. He was an aristocratic Venetian, a friar of the Franciscan Order, and a scholar of considerable reputation. He was also active in the political life of Venice for which he undertook several diplomatic assignments. In 1525 he published *De Harmonia Mundi*, a book in which he integrated Pico's Christian Kabbalah, new Hebrew sources available from Spanish refugees and his own Franciscan mysticism. In this work, we find such concepts as hierarchy of worlds, the plan of a building being used as the model of the universe, an astrological frame of reference, and man considered as the microcosm of the universal macrocosm. More important, Giorgi also makes the Monas, the Divine One, the central focus of his work. This Franciscan, who was a participant in the main stream of Italian political and artistic life, was also in the main stream of Hermetic/Kabbalistic thought which he proposed as a basis of Catholic doctrinal reform. He also influenced the German Humanists, and was of great importance in Elizabethan England.

These early Italian followers of the Hermetic/Kabbalistic tradition were Catholics seeking to revitalise the Catholic Church by means of an infusion of a Classical mystical tradition. We can find a similar turn of mind in Germany in the work of Johannes Reuchlin, a Humanist scholar who produced two books in the tradition of Christianised Kabbalah. The second, *De Arte Cabalistica*, was published in 1517. The work is important as the first complete treatment of Jewish mysticism to be written by a non-Jew, and was to become a fundamental work for Christian Kabbalists. The appearance of the book in the same year that Luther posted his theses on the church door in Wittenberg associates

Reuchlin with the start of the Reformation. Unlike Luther, who was proposing radical changes in the Church's doctrine, Reuchlin's reform sought to provide a virile replacement for the sterile scholastic approach to Catholic theology. Cornelius Agrippa seems, in the light of modern scholarship, to have had a point of view and an objective very similar to that of Reuchlin. Agrippa is important for three reasons. First, he was a Humanist, and is known to have been in England in 1510 and associated with Thomas More, John Colet and the beginnings of English Humanism. Second, he wrote *De Occulta Philosophia* which presents Kabbalah in a Christian perspective similar to that of Reuchlin and Pico. Agrippa described himself as an 'Erasmian' and 'obedient to the Church'; he is certainly not an atheist but rather a preacher of idealistic reform in the context of the Hermetic/Kabbalistic tradition. The third thing to note about Agrippa is that he is popularly remembered as the archetypal black magician and conjurer of demons, and until recently he has been considered by scholars to be unworthy of serious consideration. This reputation is based largely on the writings of Counter-Reformation authors, and particularly on the work of the Jesuit, Martin del Rio; these are hardly unbiased sources. The quite different picture of Agrippa which is emerging from contemporary research suggests that assassination of character was commonplace in the sixteenth century. It is important to recognise this, as it seems likely that the same thing happened to the English Christian Kabbalist, John Dee.

The Renaissance came late to England, and the Hermetic/Kabbalistic tradition had already become well developed and established on the Continent by the time Elizabeth I ascended to the throne. Among the courtiers who surrounded Elizabeth were a number of men who were very much involved with that body of thought. Among these was John Dee who appears to have had a great deal more influence on the thinking of the English Renaissance than has been generally recognised. Until recently historians have not given John Dee serious consideration because his reputation is that of a credulous Renaissance magician who died in poverty and was deluded by his own efforts to conjure demons. It is true that Dee fell on hard times toward the end of his life, but it is also clear that much of his bad fortune was due to the fearful, superstitious attitudes of James I. Dee's unsavoury reputation is largely due to the work of Merc Casaubon who appears to have written a destructive and heavily biased book, some forty years after Dee's death, in order to achieve objectives of his own. For material which reestablishes Dee's reputation, see Peter J. French, *John Dee* (Routledge & Kegan Paul, 1972). Dee is of interest to us because he epitomises the thinking which characterised sixteenth-century England.

Until 1583, when he left England for a tour of the Continent, John Dee was one of the most highly respected English scholars, an influential advisor to Elizabeth, and closely associated with many of the most powerful people in the land, the same people who were responsible for the English Renaissance. His library, which is acknowledged to have been the greatest in England at the time, contained nearly four thousand items, and was frequently visited by the most influential men of the period. Although much of his writing related to applied mathematics and navigation, his library is known to have contained Hermetic/Kabbalistic documents including *De Harmonia Mundi* and *De Occulta Philosophia*. Almost all his own work reflects his profound interest in the subject and shows the influence of Agrippa, Reuchlin and particularly Giorgi. The essence of John Dee's thought appears to be contained in his famous Preface to the English edition of Euclid, published in 1570. This is a thoroughly neo-platonic work with many quotations from Pico della Mirandola. It uses the Kabbalistic cosmology of Agrippa and gives fundamental priority to the Monas, the One, as the representation of Divinity. We have seen this last theme in Giorgi's work; and for Dee, who saw the Divine Presence pervading the Universe, it was to become the single idea, central to all his work. Dee was by no means the only member of the English intelligentsia to be interested in the Hermetic/Kabbalistic tradition; and if he was influenced by the work on the Continent, he also affected the views of his colleagues. He is known to have been an important member of Sidney's circle; Chapman, Spenser and Shakespeare all show evidence of a familiarity with his ideas and with *Hermetica* in general. So also do Bacon, Milton, Fludd and later Elias Ashmole.

Dee's view of the world, which is coming to be recognised in many ways as typical of the Renaissance philosophers of his school, is a provocative one. He seemed to see the universe as a sort of spectrum of phenomena with the Deity, the universal source, at one extreme and extending through 'celestial' and 'planetary' realms to gross materiality at the other. He was convinced that man could operate within this spectrum of phenomena to produce useful and beneficial effects; and the interest in magic, which occupied Dee and many (but not all) Renaissance thinkers, derived from this conviction. Magic appears to have had a somewhat different meaning to Dee and his colleagues than it does today. They seem not to make the same distinction between material, planetary and celestial worlds; and operations in any of them were considered to be 'magical'. Thus devices which we would call mechanical or hydraulic were termed examples of 'mechanical magic'. In spite of the general interest in magic among prominent scholars of the period, there were those who studied the Hermetic/Kabbalistic tradition while avoiding magic altogether. Indeed, Kabbalah in its pure form is very strict in its opposition to the use of magical practices to achieve one's own ends. Since the Craft evolved in an era when magical concepts were prominent in contemporary thought, we can expect it to have some position on the subject. As we examine the symbolic structure we will find that Masons are instructed to leave magic alone. It is also interesting to recall that C. G. Jung has pointed out that much Renaissance thought, particularly in the area of alchemy, is relevant to contemporary psychology. It may be that additional research will reveal that 'planetary magic' was a primitive research into psychology and what we call paranormal phenomena today. Peter French has called the Hermetic/Kabbalistic revival the 'dawn of the scientific age' (*ibid.*, p. 86). If that be so, it seems strange that our science-based society should be so ignorant of the subject, and we should give attention to its decline.

As one might expect, the Hermetic/Kabbalistic tradition did not prosper in Continental Europe during the Counter-Reformation. When the Council of Trent defined the doctrines within which the Catholic Church would reform itself, other proposals for change (including the work of all the thinkers mentioned above) were proscribed. Even the work of such staunch believers as Francesco Giorgi, which had been acceptable as late as 1545, was censored. In the years following 1600 many other followers of the Hermetic/Kabbalistic school were burned either by the Inquisition itself, the Catholic (or Protestant) armies participating in the Thirty Years' War, or in the witch-scares, which were used as an instrument of policy to eliminate heretics. The situation became much worse for the Hermetic school when, in 1614, Isaac Casaubon, using his newly developed Humanist technique of critical scholarship, established the correct date of the *Hermetica* as second or third century AD. Although a powerful interest in Hermetic material remained, one could no longer use the notion of Hermes Trismegistus as a pagan prophet of Christianity as a defence against heresy, and the risks attending the study of Hermetic material increased markedly.

The situation was rather different in England, which was beyond the reach of the Inquisition. As we have seen, interest in the

Hermetic/Kabbalistic tradition continued more openly. In the mid-seventeenth century Elias Ashmole's writings show that he was thoroughly conversant with Dee's work and concerns (and that he shared them himself), and Newton's interests in the mystical traditions are well known. Still, England was by no means entirely free of conflict and religious prejudice. In the mid-seventeenth century the Civil War was an actual presence, witch crazes were a distinct possibility (indeed, an occasional event), and the conflicts between Catholic and Protestant monarchs were the reality of living memory. It seems likely that the founders of the Royal Society chose to give their attention to the physical sciences where differences of opinion could be resolved by the results of experiments in the laboratory, and to ignore the more philosophical considerations which had led to conflict before. If the Royal Society had embraced the entire spectrum of Hermetic/Kabbalistic endeavour (which its charter is certainly framed to accommodate) one might speculate that psychology would have developed much earlier than it did and the conflict between science and the Church might have been avoided entirely. As it happened, the nature of time determined that the physical world was to be examined openly and other realms ('planetary' and 'celestial') were to be investigated privately – in the safety of one's own group of friends.

This brief overview of Renaissance thought and the Hermetic/Kabbalistic tradition omits many facets of the subject; for example, alchemy and the Rosicrucian movement are not mentioned at all. It certainly does not 'prove', through the tenuous connection of Elias Ashmole, that Freemasonry is a Mystery tradition. It does introduce a concept which is not part of general knowledge, but which is becoming increasingly clear to serious historians: that the Hermetic/Kabbalistic tradition was a mode of thought which was fundamental to the Renaissance and widely accepted throughout Europe at the time. It also reveals the frame of mind that was prevalent in England during the period and among the people who would have been the originators of the Speculative Craft. On this basis, we will turn to one of the original works of this tradition to find a context within which to interpret the Craft's symbolism.

3 COSMOLOGY

'... from a point to a line, from a line to a superficies, and from a superficies to a solid' is a phrase familiar to every Mason above the rank of Fellowcraft. But here we take the concept not from the Lecture of the Second Degree, but from the *Fons Vitae* written by the Spanish Kabbalist, Solomon ibn Gabirol. Ibn Gabirol, who lived and worked in Malaga around the middle of the eleventh century, was one of the first philosophers to teach neo-platonism on the continent of Europe. He was also instrumental in reformulating the Jewish Mystical tradition, which had been up until that time essentially devotional in its approach, into the metaphysical structure which was to emerge later as Spanish Kabbalah. The Geometric progression mentioned in the quotation is a neo-platonic image which was widely used by Kabbalists in medieval Spain to describe the process by which the relative universe comes into existence. Although this concept is not introduced into the Craft's symbolism until the Second Degree, we will introduce it here because it typifies the Hermetic/Kabbalistic cosmology which, as we have seen, was of importance in Renaissance thought. It thus forms a background for our consideration of the Craft's symbolic structure.

The Jewish tradition is unusually reticent when it comes to talking about God. 'God is God, and what is there to compare with God?' is a rabbinical quotation which describes the traditional attitude pretty well. This cautious turn of mind seems to be derived from the idea that if one assigns an attribute to God, one implies that God lacks the opposite attribute. For example, if one says 'God is merciful' one might suggest that in his mercy God might omit to administer justice. But the notion of a God who is not just is inconsistent with an infinite God, which is equally unacceptable. The solution to this problem is not to try to assign attributes to God at all. We cannot properly even assign the attribute of existence to God because existence is a concept which we can understand, discuss, define (or at least agree on the differences between our definitions). We can hold the concept of existence in our heads, and to assign such a limited quality to God is inconsistent with his limitless nature. God is God and is considered to be beyond even existence. In Hebrew, the word for God is Ayin, which means No Thing and also its complement, Ayin Sof, which means Without End. That, for us, is almost all that can be known about God.

There is a difficulty with this sort of thinking, however, because a limitless God must infuse all existence and, indeed, the history of human religious experience suggests that God does just that. This difficulty was resolved by the idea of the relative universe. The oral tradition has it that 'God wished to behold God' and to this end the Boundlessness which is God withdrew from a dimensionless dot, to create a void within which something might exist. That something was to be the relative universe which is the mirror within which 'God will behold God'. The void was the first thing to exist. Into this void, the Will of God projected itself as several principles – there are ten in the Kabbalistic system. These 'Divine Principles', 'The Garments of God', 'The Faces of God', 'The Divine Potencies', as they are variously called, organised themselves into a specific relationship which contained, in potential, all the universe which was to come into being, together with the laws by which that universe was to be governed. This set of related principles which exists next to the Deity is called, in Hebrew, Azilut which means 'to stand near' and is said to be the 'Image of God', the 'Glory of God', the Divine World. This Divine World of Azilut is not a world as we know it. It is a world composed entirely of Consciousness. It is timeless, in the sense that there is no time there. It exists so long as the Holy One wills it to exist, thus to us it is eternal. In the Classical, four-element universe which is common to most ancient Middle Eastern cultures, this world of pure consciousness was represented by light or fire, and in our geometric progression it is represented by the Point.

The world of Azilut, the Image of God, is sometimes called Adam Kadmon, the Primordial Man. The illustration reproduced as Figure 1 is about as close to an anthropomorphic representation of God as Judaism ever gets. It is called 'Ha Shem Ha Meforash', the Special Name, and is the same Divine Name which appears on the (Harris) Second Degree Tracing Board, but here it is arranged in vertical form. When displayed in this form it is said to represent Adam Kadmon, the Primordial Man, and from it we can derive some of the laws by which the emerging universe is to be governed.

The first is the Law of Unity. Although the diagram is composed of various components they form a single, coherent, complete thing – the Special Name. Next come the Law of Opposites and the Rule of Three, both of which are represented in the Divine Name by the three columns formed by the vertical strokes in the characters. The Law of Opposites is implied by the two outside columns. The right-hand column is composed of bold straight strokes and is said to be active, creative, expansive, merciful and masculine. Left to its own devices this expansive principle would dissipate itself into the void. It is, however, complemented by the left-hand column, which is composed of graceful, yielding strokes, said to be passive, containing, conserving, severe and feminine. By itself the passive principle would implode because it is entirely constraining. These two outside columns contain in potential

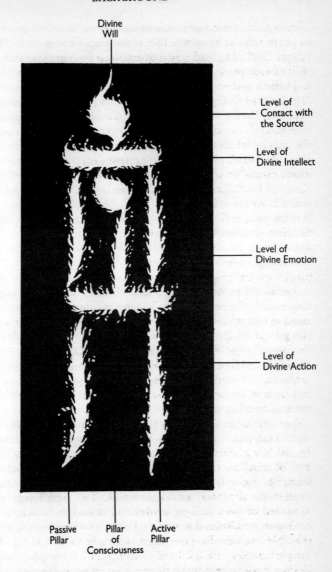

Figure 1 *Ha Shem Ha Meforash, the Special Name*
(By permission of Zevben Shimon Haleve)

all the pairs of contrasting phenomena in the emerging universe. They are to be held in balance by a mediating agency implied by the central Column of Consciousness, in the middle of the Name. Its task is to hold the other two (and the entire universe) in dynamic balance. The name is composed of four characters. They represent four levels within the Divine World. These are called the Levels of Divine Action, Divine Emotion, Divine Intellect and a Contact with the Deity and are seen as the source of the four worlds which will comprise the relative universe. We should not fall into the trap of thinking that the laws derive from the shape of the Divine Name. The Kabbalistic tradition is based on the experience of these laws by those who formulated it, and the Hebrew language and alphabet are said to have been designed to facilitate the transmission of the tradition. Thus, the Special Name in its vertical form should be regarded as an *aide-mémoire* written in a language designed specifically for the construction of such sacred models. The letters in this form represent the laws, but are not to be thought of as the source of the laws.

This Divine world of Azilut is pure, innocent and perfect because of its proximity to the Deity. While all things exist in Azilut in potential, they cannot manifest. Nothing happens in this world because it is static, unchanging, perfect. In order that the relative universe can accomplish its task of reflecting God, Adam Kadmon must experience all things; and to facilitate that process a whole new world, the World of Creation, comes into existence. Heretofore, we have been working with the oral tradition, but with the process of Creation we move to the written tradition which is contained in the Torah – the first five books of the Bible. The first chapter of Genesis starts with the words 'In the beginning God created . . .', in Hebrew 'Berashit bara Elohim . . .' and in these first words we have a contradiction which we must resolve. Elohim is a plural form, meaning literally 'many Gods', but Judaism is a militantly monotheistic religion. The resolution of this conflict points us back to the oral tradition. The word Elohim refers to the ten principles, the 'Faces' or 'Garments of God' which were originally emanated to form the Divine World. Creation is seen to be effected by the agency of Divine Will operating through these ten principles. Thus, the World of Creation is seen as springing forth from the centre of the Divine World.

The word Creation has a more precise, and therefore more restricted meaning in this context than it has in ordinary (even ordinary religious) usage. Here it refers specifically and exclusively to this second world which springs from the primordial world of Adam Kadmon. This World of Creation unfolds according to the description in the first chapter of Genesis. As the first world of separation from the static perfection of Divinity, it is a world of change. It is the beginning of time and space, of good and evil, and of all the other relative concepts which comprise the universe in which we live. Creation – that is, the second world – unfolds according to the pattern established in the Divine World of Azilut, and it is completed in seven days – or steps – but again, we are not speaking of the ordinary physical world with which we are familiar. As the world of Emanation is a world of Consciousness, the World of Creation is a world of Spirit, of ideas, of essences, of energy. It is Heaven in Jewish terminology; the Celestial world in Renaissance terms. The World of the Spirit is governed by the same set of laws as those which we observed in the Divine World. It has unity, in that it is a consistent whole, it has active and passive aspects which are co-ordinated by a conscious element, and it has four levels; action, emotion, intellect and a contact with the source – in this case the Creator at the centre of the Divine World. In the Kabbalistic tradition, this world is inhabited (largely) by archangels who perform the active and passive celestial functions. In the classical four-element universe it is the World of Air. It is the Line in the Craft's geometric progression.

When Creation was complete a third world derived from its centre in the same way that Creation was derived from the midst of Divinity. The second chapter of Genesis has a real similarity to the first and some scholars pass it off as repetition for emphasis. It is important to note, however, that whereas in Genesis 1, the world is 'created', the operative verb in Genesis 2 is 'formed'. The repetitive nature of the text tells us that the same laws which are found in the Divine and Spiritual Worlds will also operate in this new world. But there is a world of difference between Creation and Formation. The World of Formation is the 'Planetary' world in Renaissance terminology. In Kabbalistic terminology it is called Paradise and Eden, and it is inhabited by angels. Here, with the World of Forms, we have reached a level to which we can relate our ordinary experiences. In contemporary terminology we would call this world the psyche. It is the realm of Archetype and Symbol. In the Classical Greek idiom, it is the world of the gods whose adventures depict the dynamics of the psyche in symbolic, mythical form. Its ever-changing images are represented by the element Water in the four-element universe. This World of Formation is symbolised by the Superficies in the Craft's geometric progression and it is the world which is represented by the symbolic structure of the Masonic Lodge.

By a similar process a fourth world, the World of Action comes into being from the midst of Paradise. This is the physical world, and includes 'space' all the phenomena which are the subject for investigation by the physical sciences. It is called 'Earth' in the terminology of the four-element universe, and the Solid in the geometric progression. It is the world which mankind entered when he was sent out of Eden (in Paradise) and given 'coats of skin' (bodies) – an event of which we will have a great deal to say in due course.

We can represent this scheme, to a limited extent, in a diagram such as the one shown in Figure 2. Each world is represented by a circle, each being a successively grosser reflection of the world above. The uppermost point on each circumference touches the centre of the circle above, reminding us that the source of each world is the centre of the next higher world. The worlds interpenetrate each other, as do the elements which represent them. Thus, Light penetrates Air, Air dissolves in Water and Water saturates Earth. Common human experience verifies the last of these examples: the human psyche seems to permeate the body, but it is quite clear that the psyche is not a physical thing. It is also a common experience for human beings to realise that the body and psyche are two different things, that is, to realise, 'This is my body. It is mine, but it is not me.' The dimension which is represented by the vertical axis of the diagram is the 'Dimension of Consciousness'. At the bottom is found the grossest materiality from which consciousness rises in gradual stages to the most refined awareness of Divinity at the top. To the Kabbalist this model represents the entire relative universe, the whole of existence. It is the 'that' in the Divine Utterance 'I am that I am', which brings it into existence and holds it there.

The oral tradition has it that all the universe, except mankind itself, was created, formed and made in the three lower worlds. Human beings, it is said, existed as cells (so to speak) in Adam Kadmon – were made in the Image of God – whence they descend as individual Divine Sparks through the three lower worlds. In the process of this descent each Divine Spark is enwrapped in a Spirit as it enters the World of Creation, the spirit is enclothed in a Soul as it descends into the World of Formation (psyche), and finally, it acquires a body when it incarnates. Here, in the farthest remove of physical existence, these individual human beings start the long journey back to their Divine origin. This is the task of the human being; as the scriptures have it 'for this you were called forth, created, formed and made'. When each cell of

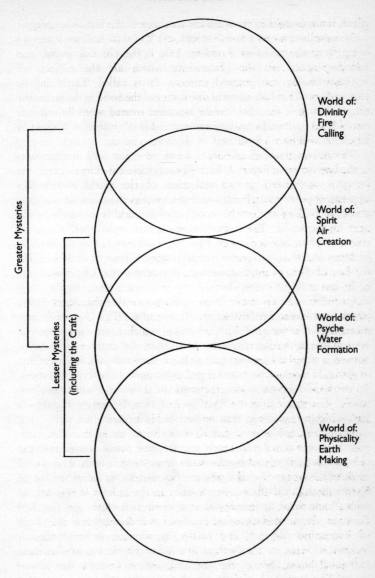

Figure 2

Adam Kadmon has returned to its original place, Adam Kadmon will be again complete, as he was in the beginning. But he will no longer be innocent and naive, rather he will have the richness of all experience, at which time God will behold God in the Mirror of Existence.

The cosmology outlined above gives a reasonable, if rather simplistic view of the Kabbalistic scheme of the universe set out in the contemporary idiom. (For a more complete treatment of this subject, also in the contemporary idiom, see Z'Ev ben Shimon Halevi, *A Kabbalistic Universe*, Ryder, 1977). The assiduous reader can relate it to the narrative in the Book of Genesis, and this will be the basic cosmology to which we will refer throughout. The human being fits into this scheme of things in a unique way because he can, if he chooses to do so, operate consciously in all four worlds – a capacity which is possessed by no other being. To be conscious in all four worlds is the subject taught by the Mysteries, no matter what their idiom or terminology for this concept may be. From this point of view, the Craft of Freemasonry is said to be a Lesser Mystery, since it deals with the World of Formation, that is, with the psyche, the more elementary part of this process.

Before we leave this cosmology, we must touch on one more concept which is inherent in the scheme. The lecture in the Second Degree describes Geometry as 'a science whereby we find out the contents of bodies unmeasured by comparing them with those already measured'. This is a statement of the principle of man the microcosm of the universe. It is a principle which is put even more succinctly as, 'As above, so below'. We have seen that the same set of laws are said to apply in each of the four worlds – they simply operate differently at different levels. We have seen also that human beings have, within themselves, each of these levels or worlds. The tradition has it that there is a resonance between events in each of the worlds and that an event in the physical world causes analogous events in the upper worlds. This idea of resonance between worlds is the principle which underlies the use of ceremony and ritual. It can be verified easily – at least for the case of resonance between the physical and psychological worlds – by common experience. One has only to view a well conducted military ceremony, say the Trooping of the Colour or the May Day parade in Red Square, and by observing one's own response, to feel the reaction in the psyche as martial feeling and national pride wells up in response to the event in the physical world. If the same person will watch the Monarch place a wreath at the Cenotaph or attend quietly the funeral of a stranger at a village church, he will learn quickly how ceremonies can be structured to produce specific and quite discrete psychological events. These are simple, straightforward exercises conducted with commonly found ceremonies to verify the fact that suitably designed rituals produce definite psychological states. Quite subtle rituals can be constructed using this principle of resonance between the worlds, and the ceremonies of the Craft are designed along these lines. They have been constructed with great care to produce psychological experiences which provide the candidate with an insight into his psyche, while at the same time protecting him from the risks which are associated with exploration of the World of Formation. Here we see one of the principal reasons why the Craft is so very reluctant to introduce changes in its symbolic structure. Well meaning changes to the ritual introduced without a knowledge of their effect in the upper worlds could have a very detrimental impact on the participants in the ceremonies.

This brief sketch of Kabbalistic cosmology provides us with the frame of reference we require. It is a fair view, in modern terms, of the conceptual framework of the Renaissance citizen who was interested in his interior growth. With this model of the four worlds and their interrelationships in the back of our minds we will look in a little more detail at some contemporary models of the World of Formation, the psyche, the field of study embraced by the Craft's symbolic structure.

4 PSYCHOLOGY

We said in the preceding section that the Masonic Lodge can be considered to be a model of the Psychological World. More precisely, it is a model of the human psyche, the human being as he exists in the World of Formation. In this sense we may think of the Craft as an antique, God-orientated, psychology – as a sort of science of human mental processes set out in a symbolic structure which may appear quaint by modern standards but which is consistent and valid when considered in its own terms. We might think of its originators as practitioners of a disciple which we would describe today as a branch of the academic field called Consciousness Research. However, if we are going to consider the Craft as a sort of psychology (as we will be doing throughout this book), we must be very careful in several respects. We need to understand clearly the differences between the theories, aims and attitudes of contemporary psychology and those of the Craft before we begin to examine the parallels between the two.

In the first place, psychology as it is practised in the twentieth century has a distinctly therapeutic context in the public view. This association of psychology with the medical profession is probably inevitable. Our materialistic social and intellectual paradigm which emerged during the Industrial Revolution did not have much place for the psyche, and it was through treating physical symptoms of psychological origin that physicians first came to give any attention to the psyche at all. Thus, the two prominent pioneers in the field, Freud and Jung, were both medical practitioners; and our society has come to be interested in psychological matters through accounts of their psychotherapeutic activities. In fact, this blurring in the public awareness of the distinction between psychotherapy (which is a medical concern) and psychology (which is a general knowledge of our mental processes) is an inconvenience for practitioners in both fields and it is common to find this distinction made in the literature on the subject. The Craft is in a somewhat different situation. It derives from a society whose paradigm was not materialistic. It was a paradigm which had a fundamentally psychological orientation, a paradigm in which knowledge was based on a 'psychological reality' rather than a 'physical reality'. Psychological development, as an intellectual concept, was as normal as physical development. The psychological models of the time, of which the Craft offers an example, were designed to facilitate this normal psychological growth. Thus the first caution of which we must be aware: when we consider the Craft as a psychology we must understand it to be an approach to normal human development; we must not confuse it with a means for treating psychological disorders.

The second notion of which we must be careful is to avoid the temptation to think of the Craft as '*only* another form of psychology'. Freemasonry and contemporary psychology have much in common because they both deal with the same area of human experience, but each approaches that area in its own way, and each has different objectives. Psychology as a twentieth-century scientific discipline is atheistic (in the strict sense of the word) and its objectives have to do with people living normal lives in a materialistic society. Normal, in this sense, is a statistical concept; and has to do with behaviour which is common to most people in the society. Contemporary psychology does not use 'normal' in its other context, 'behaviour in accordance with design criteria', because it does not recognise the existence of a 'designer' nor can it identify the 'design criteria'. To say that another way, psychology as a scientific discipline does not acknowledge the concept of God or Divine purpose for mankind. The Craft, in contrast, is a psychology which acknowledges the primacy of God and envisions a psychological development in which the individual fulfulls his potential in order best to serve the Divine Will.

In the third place, we should not be led to believe that, because the Craft's psychological concepts are expressed in terms which are quaint by modern scientific standards, they are outmoded or no longer useful. The field of psychology has not advanced as rapidly in the last ninety years as its 'hard science' counterparts; and, in general, psychology has not lived up to the promise which it seemed to offer when it first appeared around the turn of the century. There is a real possibility that contemporary scientific techniques might be better adapted to psychological investigation by the addition of some 'old-fashioned' concepts and practices. (This is actually happening. Some psychologists and physicians are turning their attention to research into such areas as paranormal phenomena, near-death experience and regression to pre-birth experience. Such research is very difficult in the context of the scientific paradigm. The progress in this area will be slow, but initial results provide evidence which concurs with the old, 'mystical' world view). On the other hand, contemporary psychology has compiled a vast amount of observational data, and a great deal of serious thought by dedicated and conscientious scientists lies behind the current theories which have been formulated as a result of the research. It would be arrogant and foolish simply to dismiss this work. To the contrary, if our view of the Craft as a psychology be an accurate one, we should be able to embrace these findings (at least in a general way) and we may expect to find substantial areas of correspondence between the contemporary theories and our interpretation of the Craft's symbolic structure. As we will see, those correspondences do exist, and we will make a good deal of use of modern psychological concepts where they are appropriate. Because of the different world views outlined above; however, we will start with some different assumptions and arrive at some different conclusions. We should not feel badly about these differences; contemporary psychology is, itself, by no means a homogeneous body of theory. In the paragraphs that follow we will introduce the major concepts of the two most influential contemporary psychologists, Freud and Jung, and for our purposes we will require only their most basic ideas. Although these two theories are quite different, we will use concepts from both. As we will see in the course of our examination of Masonry, the differences which so separated the two men may very well derive from the fact that they were each studying a different part of the same thing.

Freud

Freudian psychology was formulated, as much as possible, within the context of the scientific method. Although debates have continued into the 1980s about the validity of psychology's claim to be a science, it is certainly true that Freud did his best to establish the discipline on a scientific footing and that his successors have continued those efforts. There has been, in recent years, a proposal to distinguish between Freud's clinical theories and his philosophical work on the origin and purpose of the mind and to abandon the latter in favour of the former. As a result of these efforts Freud's work has been the psychological theory most acceptable to our materialistic twentieth-century society and, not surprisingly, the least comparable to Masonry.

In Freud's model the human psyche comprises three levels, which he calls the id, the ego and the super-ego. Two of these levels, the id and the super-ego, reside in a domain called 'the unconscious', while the third, the ego, comprises the conscious portion of the mind. Freud considers the id to be the basic and most real level of the psyche. It is in intimate contact with the body, is the residence of the instincts, and is the source of all the psyche's energy. The id operates on the pleasure principle. That is, it acts to seek pleasure through the release of tension which the id perceives as pain. Thus when a bright light is shined into a person's eyes he blinks, relieving the pain. This reflex is the sort of action which is within the scope of the id. While there are a great many tensions which can be resolved by such direct reflexes, it is really a very primitive sort of behaviour and the id is described as being infantile, amoral and non-ethical.

While reflex is a satisfactory response to many situations, a far greater number of tension-producing situations demand more sophisticated behaviour if the tension is to be relieved. Hunger, for example, produces tension which cannot be relieved by reflex action. A hungry person must identify, locate, acquire and eat food before the tension is relieved. Moreover he must acquire the food in a way which does not produce greater pain or tension. This more sophisticated behaviour is the task of the ego, which evolves out of the id during childhood as the child learns to cope with increasingly complex situations. The ego performs several tasks: it builds, and stores in memory, images of things in the physical world which can be used to meet its needs; it postpones actions to relieve tension until the actions are appropriate (that is until they will not produce a worse situation);

and it formulates plans to release tension in an acceptable way. To state these functions in terms of the example of a hungry person, the ego remembers what food is, which things are good to eat and which are poisonous; it does not steal food (at least, not in the presence of a policeman) and it arranges circumstances (such as a purchase or barter) to acquire food and eat it in peace. All of these processes are what we call 'thinking'. In Freudian terms the ego operates using the 'reality principle' to relate the individual's instinctual needs to the constraints of the physical world. Thus the ego thinks, plans and tolerates tension until it can achieve pleasure in a realistic manner. The ego is not (necessarily) primitive or infantile, but it is amoral – seeking rewards and avoiding punishment.

The super-ego, which like the id is in that portion of the psyche of which the individual is unconscious, is the agency which introduces morality into the personality. Freud suggests that as the individual develops through childhood he receives rewards (physical, such as food or privilege, or psychological, such as love or approval) and punishments (physical, such as deprivation, or psychological, such as disapproval) for his behaviour. These childhood experiences are forgotten in time, but are stored in the unconsciousness as associations of reward with certain kinds of behaviour and punishment with others. They develop into the super-ego which has two facets: conscience, which defines wrong and ego-ideal, which defines right. Through this process of rewards and punishments, administered by parents, teachers and others in authority, the child learns how he is expected to behave (not how his parents actually behave but what behaviour they think is right and wrong); and by reference to his super-ego the individual can regulate his behaviour in accordance with his parents', and later his society's expectations. Ultimately, the function of the super-ego is to enable the individual to relate to society.

Freud recognised in his later work that there were two general classes of instincts which reside in the id and put energy into the psyche; those which tend to promote life and those which tend to cause death. The former group were termed (by Freud) as Libido, and the latter have been called (by his successors) Mortido. The general business of Freudian psychology (and psychotherapy) is the study of the interaction of these constructive and destructive instinctual energies as they are exchanged between the various structural elements of the model described above. In particular, it is concerned with the role of the ego as the central feature, conscious essence, and controlling agency of the psyche. We can see that

Freud's psychology is very much orientated toward clinical evidence and environmental determinism, and is quite devoid of mystical or even metaphysical speculation.

Jung

Jung was several years younger than Freud and while his early career was profoundly influenced by his predecessor, his mature work was quite different. He felt much less constrained to produce work which was acceptable to the conventional scientific community. Jung's concepts include reference to a wide variety of classical, primitive and historical materials which might appear (at first) to be quite unrelated to his clinical experience. For this reason Jung has often been accused of being fuzzy, of dabbling in metaphysics; and it is only relatively recently that his work has begun to have a growing acceptance. Like Freud, Jung recognised the importance of the unconscious portion of the psyche. He could not, however, accept the overwhelming priority which his older colleague attached to instinct (and particularly the sex instinct) as the sole causal agency in the development of the psyche. Like Freud, Jung regarded the analysis of dreams as one of the most valuable devices for examining the unconscious, but his dream analysis led him to a very different model of the psyche. According to Jung's concept the individual's psyche is whole to begin with. Psychological development is a process of bringing the components of the psyche into consciousness and synthesising them. Jung's view of the psyche consists of three levels, the individual consciousness, the personal unconscious and the collective unconscious.

There are four functions potentially available to the individual consciousness – thinking, feeling, sensation and intuition. The first two are rational in the sense that they involve ordering things; thinking orders them by analysis, feeling orders them by value. The second two are said to be irrational functions in that they do not involve judgment or reasoning; sensation involves perception of reality (internal or external), intuition is perception of the potential inherent in an event, sometimes from the unconscious as with a 'hunch' or 'just knowing'. The individual may also have two attitudes: extraversion, which is an orientation towards events outside one's self, and introversion, which is a concern with one's interior life. The ego is the conscious part of the psyche and in this respect is the supervisor of day-to-day psychological activity. It has, among others, the task of selecting the phenomena (thought, memory, perception or feeling) which will be permitted into consciousness. The criteria for selection and rejection depend upon which function and attitude is dominant and upon the extent to which the person is self-possessed. This selectivity of the ego is an essential defence for the psyche which would otherwise be overwhelmed by input of one sort or another. The ego has the task of relating the individual to his physical and social environment. One of the principal adaptive devices used by the ego is the persona (from the Greek word for mask), which is the façade which the ego presents to the world. Far from being hypocritical, the persona permits one to fit into the demands of social situations while maintaining one's individuality. A person may use several personae, one at home, another at work, a third for his time at the pub. Each permits him to relate differently to different situations. In managing these personae the ego provides for a continuity of consciousness so that one knows one's self to be the same person while exhibiting different personae in different situations.

The personal unconscious contains material which has been conscious at some time, and has since been forgotten or repressed, together with impressions of experiences which the ego did not, or could not, allow into consciousness. It contains a sort of comprehensive record of the individual's experience. Material can generally be recalled from the personal unconscious as, for example, when one remembers a telephone number of which one is conscious only when it is being used. The personal unconscious also contains what Jung called 'complexes'. A complex is a cluster of attitudes, feelings and behaviour patterns which have become associated around a common element which may be any event or object in the individual's history. People are usually unaware of their complexes, although they generally have profound effect on the person's behaviour. They may be detrimental, such as a complex which regards money as evil and causes the individual to reject it, live in poverty, and condemn all commercial activity; or advantageous as in the case of an inventor who is driven to pursue his practice with single-mindedness and finally produces a device which makes a great advance in the well being of society. In the exploration of the personal unconscious one encounters the 'Self'. Jung uses the term to describe a principle which pulls together and integrates the several components of the psyche. It usually remains beyond the threshold of consciousness only to emerge, if at all, in middle or later life, after the other elements of the psyche have become reasonably well identified and disciplined.

The collective unconscious is a part of the psyche which does not depend upon individual experience. It is shared by all members of the human race and contains material of which the individual may never have been conscious. The collective unconscious consists of prototype images; that is, of images which provide the basis upon which similar psychological experiences will be built. These primordial images, which Jung called archetypes, consist only of 'form without content, representative merely of the possibility of a certain perception and action'. An example will help clarify this point. There is an archetype in the collective unconscious of the Hero. It contains the essence of heroism and each individual human being has access to the hero archetype. The particular image which any one individual will have of a hero will depend upon his experience with heroic individuals in his own life. There are a vast number of archetypes: concepts such as birth, death, mother and father; objects such as rivers, stones, animals; artifacts such as candles, swords, rings and boxes may all be archetypes. In fact, Jung conceived that there is an archetype for each basic human situation. In studying the archetypes which he encountered in the course of his professional practice Jung drew on material from anthropology as well as from Classical, medieval and Renaissance literature. He spent substantial time investigating the symbolic structure of alchemy, and was probably the first modern investigator to recognise that much medieval and Renaissance thought, which our society usually calls superstition, is actually a description of psychological processes expressed in an unfamiliar symbolic form.

Some archetypes are of such basic importance as to have a central role in Jung's theories. Some we have already noted: the persona, which we have seen is the conforming archetype; and the Self, the archetype of integration and co-ordination. Others include the animus and anima and the shadow.

All theories of the psyche treat the subject of sexuality and Jung approaches it through the archetypes of the animus and anima. Each human psyche is, in Jung's view, complete; and like the body which contains the chemistry of both sexes, the psyche contains the essential psychological qualities of both sexes, male and female, animus and anima respectively. In men the animus is identified with the ego, while the anima is concealed; the reverse is true with women. The nature of a man's anima and his relationship to it will determine the nature of his relationship with the women he meets in the world, and the reverse situation is true for women.

The shadow is the archetype which contains a great deal of

instinctual material, as well as aspects of the individual's own psyche which he would prefer not to acknowledge. The process of fitting in to society causes many people to put their powerful instincts and strong emotions out of their consciousness and suppress them by exercising a strong persona. This suppressed material which one chooses not to acknowledge about one's self resides in the shadow where it is always ready to break out into manifestation. Frequently people project the contents of their own shadow on others, assigning to them the faults which they cannot acknowledge in themselves.

Jungian psychologists describe the psychological processes in terms of the exchange of energy between the elements in the structure outlined above. These elements may compensate for one another, oppose one another or unite to form a synthesis. Like their Freudian colleagues, the Jungians envision a development within the psyche; but the objectives are quite different. Freud envisions a strengthening of the ego so that it can cope with the situations presented by life. Jung envisions a differentiation of the many archetypes which make up the psyche by their being admitted by the ego into consciousness where they are integrated into the whole by the co-ordinating function of the Self.

This overview of the two most prominent psychological schools hardly scratches the surface of each. Indeed, it touches only upon the most basic concepts of the founders of these two schools, and ignores the development which has occurred in both theories. Our purpose here, however, is not to compare the Craft with contemporary psychology. The review above is intended only to provide us with a definition of the basic concepts to use when we discuss the symbols of the Craft. It also indicates that Freud's work, although acknowledging the importance of the unconscious, tends to concentrate on the more concrete area of conscious processes; while Jung was prepared to forego approval of the scientific community to develop more completely his theories of the unconscious and its structure. Because of this difference we will find that Jung's work is more generally parallel to the Craft's symbolism than that of Freud; but, as we have said, we will use concepts from both as we move, at last, from our survey of background material to our examination of the Craft itself.

CHAPTER 2
The Craft

1 PREREQUISITES AND MOTIVES

We have said specifically that the Mysteries are universally available, so it may seem strange to start by discussing prerequisites. It is the case, however, that one must have certain qualifications and that one will be excluded from the study of the Mysteries if one is not in possession of them. In the case of the Craft, these qualifications are set out in the ritual and a person will not be recommended for membership into a Masonic Lodge unless he meets these ritual requirements. At first glance this arrangement may seem to be unfair. We must realise, however, that the Craft is but one of many disciplines which guide their followers in interior work. As we examine the qualifications we will gain a first glimpse into the nature of the Work in general and into the process of interpreting the symbols of the Craft in particular. We will also see that anyone lacking the qualifications for the Work can acquire them if he wishes, and that the requirements are not as unfair as they may seem at first glance.

The first prerequisite for entry into any form of the Work is that the prospective candidate must believe in a Supreme Being. There are several reasons for this requirement. The course of instruction is based on understanding laws which are considered to be of Divine origin. The objective of the instruction is to bring the candidate to a conscious awareness of the presence of Divinity. Both of these notions are meaningless unless the candidate believes in some Deity in the first place. More fundamentally, the candidate is expected to commit his new found knowledge to the service of his God. A candidate who lacks this fundamental belief cannot, of course, make such a commitment and his motive for pursuing the Work must necessarily be a personally orientated one. More important still, as we will see in the pages that follow, there are stages in the course of the Work when the candidate's belief in his God is the only thing which is available to him as a guide. At these junctures one who has entered the Work depending only on his own capacities can expect to find himself in serious trouble. In the Masonic idiom, this fundamental requirement for belief in a Supreme Being is stated in exactly those terms. The name and form of the Deity (or the absence of those qualities), the scripture through which It is revealed, and manner in which It is to be worshipped are entirely outside the purview of the Craft, and are left to the discretion of the individual.

The second prerequisite is that the candidate shall be a volunteer. This is a difficult problem, in a way, because in the very real sense, the prospective candidate has no way of knowing what he is getting into. It is none the less very important. In the process of Masonic Labour the candidate will come to know himself as he is. As Robert Burns has pointed out, human beings do not, as a general rule, see themselves objectively. They rarely examine their real motivations, and they seldom acknowledge the effects which their actions have on others. The man who would be a Craftsman in the interior sense will do all these things and the task of examining one's motives and the effects of one's actions is usually unpleasant and sometimes very stressful. It is important that the individual knows very clearly that he has undertaken the experience himself. If he can blame his difficult circumstances on anyone else, he will not grow. In the Masonic idiom, this requirement for voluntary commitment is expressed in two ways: first, by the fact that membership is not solicited – one must ask to become a Mason; and second in the ritual by the Worshipful Master's repeated demand for an assurance by the candidate that his request for admission is 'of your own free will and accord'. It is important to understand the concept of voluntary commitment and unsolicited membership correctly. When someone is clearly seeking the sort of information which the Work provides it is not improper to suggest that he investigate this or that area, nor is it inappropriate to indicate that the Craft offers instruction of this sort. What is improper is to urge someone to begin an examination of himself before he himself feels he is ready to undertake the task.

The third prerequisite for the Mysteries is that the candidate shall be mature and stable. The reason for this requirement should be quite clear from the comments in the preceding paragraph, and they will become even more so as we progress to our examination of Masonic Labour. Various schools express this requirement in different ways. For example, one tradition says that the candidate should be forty years old and happily married, which is certainly a way of requiring that he has come to grips with ordinary life. The Craft expresses this requirement by specifying that the candidate be twenty-one years of age, and this rule is based – like all of the ritual – on a very specific principle. The human being is thought to develop normally according to a very definite pattern of stages consisting of approximately seven years each. From birth to age seven the child develops his concept of himself as a separate identity; from seven to thirteen he develops his mental capacities with endless games, tricks and gadgets; from fourteen to twenty, the period of adolescence, he develops the passionate side of his nature. By the time the person is twenty-one, physical and elementary mental development is complete; one is entering one's physical prime. With the turbulence of adolescence in the past, one is ready to continue the normal pattern of human growth by developing the capacities of the psyche. By whatever standard one measures it, maturity and stability are important requirements because objective examination of one's self is, at best, an unsettling experience.

The fourth, and last prerequisite for entry into any form of the Work is that one should be prepared to accept responsibility for one's behaviour. It should be clear that individual responsibility for one's actions is necessary for any kind of constructive learning about one's self, because, as long as one's circumstances are perceived as being the fault of another, a person is powerless to change his own situation. Indeed, 'they have done this to me', stated in one form or another, is the basic excuse which hinders all human progress; and 'they have done this to you' is the basic phrase which perpetuates human slavery – although it may induce people to change their masters from time to time. In the Masonic idiom the prerequisite of individual responsibility is expressed by requiring that the candidate shall be a Free Man. No one should have any difficulty with the use of freedom – the symbolism uses the word in contrast to the condition of slavery – in this context, because a slave can legitimately place responsibility for his actions on his master. However, to advance seriously – in a book written in England in the last half of the twentieth century – the notion that one must be a man in order to accept responsibility for himself is asking for trouble; and a decent respect for the sensibilities of society requires that this point be examined.

From the point of view of the Work, there is no reason why women should not participate. In fact, there are many Orders – some restricted to women and some androgenous – in which women work with great ability and effect, and some of these are said to use a Masonic organisation, ritual and symbolic structure essentially the same as the one discussed here. It is also clear, from the performance of women in government, business, science, academe, the family and the arts, that women can accept responsibility as willingly, and discharge it as ably as men; and nothing which is contained herein should be interpreted to the contrary. We must recognise, however, that we are examining a symbolic structure which was constructed in sixteenth- or seventeenth-century England. Like all symbolic structures, it uses the conventions of its time to convey its meanings. In the social situation that obtained in sixteenth-century England, women were not permitted to assume responsibility under the law, and it is from this situation that the Free Man as the symbol of one who can be responsible for himself has been derived. One can argue, with some justification, that the symbol – which is only a symbol after all – should be changed, since it is no longer appropriate; and that the Craft should admit women into the Order. One is encouraged in this argument by the undeniable fact that this particular symbol does not convey to the latter-day Mason the meaning which was originally intended. But there is more to it than that. Careful historical research is always required to interpret old symbols properly; and Freemasonry is by no means alone in respect of the need to do research for that purpose. That is not the real issue. We have seen that Freemasonry is the custodian of a symbolism which contains, at the same time, a model of the psyche and rituals which have been designed to have specific effects on the candidate at the psychological level. It is because of this consideration that the Craft has compelling reasons to resist any changes in its symbolic structure. Whether those reasons are sufficiently compelling to justify a continued refusal to admit women into the Order is a matter of opinion which will not be resolved here. It should be clear, however, that the Craft's reasons for resisting such a change are neither trivial or arbitrary.

In addition to the basic prerequisities for candidacy, the Craft looks for certain motivations in its candidates. These motives are typically sought by all traditions of interior work, and in Masonry they are expressed by the Worshipful Master's questions to the candidate immediately after his admission to the Lodge as a candidate for the First Degree. Although these questions are generally treated as the merest formality, they are, in fact, of great importance. The appropriate motives are a real desire to learn about one's self and to put that new-found knowledge to use on behalf of mankind. Furthermore, this motivation must be strong enough to impel the individual to persevere because, as we have already hinted, and as we shall see later, the Work is

difficult and at times demanding of real sacrifice. No one should enter
the Work with the idea of personal gain or without the willingness to
make whatever changes in himself the requirements of Providence,
operating through the medium of his personal experience, will demand.
There are personal gains, 'inestimable privileges' as the ritual describes
them, but they are by-products of Masonic Labours, not achievable
directly as personal objectives. Coming, as they do, early in the
Ceremony of the First Degree, the Master's questions should be regarded
as a warning by those who would look deeply into the Craft –
particularly the Master's request for a promise to persevere through the
Ceremony of the Degree. It does not require much in the way of
perseverence to complete twenty-five minutes of formal ritual,
conducted by dignified gentlemen in the congenial surroundings of a
Masonic Lodge. To persevere through the life experience which the
ceremony represents is a very different thing, as we shall see when we
discuss Masonic Labour.

Before we can do that, however, we must have some insight into the
manner in which the Craft uses its symbols to formulate its model of the
human psyche.

2 THE LODGE AS A MODEL OF THE PSYCHE

To be considered complete a model of the psyche should address three
areas: structure, which identifies the components of the psyche and their
mutual relationships; dynamics, which is concerned with the principles
by which the psyche operates; and development, which describes how
the psyche emerges and unfolds. From the developmental point of view
we have seen that the Craft is concerned specifically with development
beyond the stage called, in contemporary terms, the 'young adult'.
Apart from that limitation, the Craft presents a complete model of the
psyche in that it addresses each of those three areas. The process of
development is reflected in the candidate's progress through the three
degrees, and will unfold throughout the progress of this book. The
subjects of structure and dynamics are presented in overview in the
following sections.

Structure – The Temple

When a candidate knocks on the door of a Masonic Lodge he is
standing, symbolically, at the threshold of his own consciousness. The

Figure 3

Tyler, as we shall see when we examine the Officers of the Lodge, represents that part of the psyche which operates in the physical world using the central nervous system as its instrument. Beyond the door of the Lodge, the threshold of his consciousness, the candidate finds a 'Temple' which is said to have four levels. These are a Ground Floor, a Middle Chamber, a Holy of Holies and, residing within this last, the Divine Presence. We can sense immediately the correspondence between the levels in the Masonic Temple and the four levels which characterise each of the Worlds in our model of the cosmos. That is, within each World we saw a level of Action, Emotion and Intellect and a contact with its Source in the World above.

The first three of these levels relate directly to the three degrees of the Craft, and the nature of the activity which goes on at each level is described by the tools used by Masons of each degree. The tools of the First Degree relate to action, to shaping, to cutting and polishing; those of the Second Degree relate to judgment, to testing and proving; while those of the Third Degree relate to creativity and design.

This general plan is represented in Figure 3 in a diagram which Masons will recognise as a sort of composite Tracing Board. It is rather like a First Degree Tracing Board drawn from the perspective of a Master Mason and on it we can see the four levels described above. We can relate this diagram, in a general way, to contemporary psychology and particularly to the Jungian structural concept. Generally the Ground Floor represents the conscious and the rest of the Temple the unconscious. We can be a little more precise.

The Ground Floor represents that part of the psyche which is in immediate contact with the body and through the body with the physical world. It is the part of the psyche where the functions of thinking, feeling, sensation and intuition may be experienced. The activities of the Ground Floor are under the immediate control of the ego. In Jungian terms this is the part of the psyche called the individual consciousness. The Middle Chamber is an intermediate level in the Temple. It is not in contact with the Earth and the outside world as the Ground Floor is, nor is it open to the Heavens as is the Holy of Holies. It is, in a sense, the essence of the Temple. In terms of the individual, the Middle Chamber is his psychological essence, his soul. It is a level which is ordinarily beyond conscious awareness; and, as we have said, it has to do with emotion, with morality and judgment. Most people experience this level only when they are prompted by their conscience. Since it is the part of the psyche where experience is stored we can expect to find the super-ego described by Freud and many of the complexes identified by Jung located here. We can think of the Middle Chamber as corresponding to the Jungian personal unconscious and as the residence of the Self.

The Holy of Holies represents a level deep within the psyche which exerts profound influence on our behaviour although it is an area of which most people are rarely consciously aware. It is the area of the psyche which is in contact with the world of the Spirit in the same way that the Ground Floor is in contact with the physical world. It is an area not embraced by Freud's theories; but in Jung's terms it corresponds in a general way to the collective unconscious. The traditional description of this level is Intellect and the word is used to describe trans-personal concepts which are shared by all members of the species – comparable to Jung's archetypes.

The Divine Presence is said to reside in the Holy of Holies. The acknowledgment of this Presence, and the recognition of its influence in the life of the individual, is the feature which most distinguishes Freemasonry from conventional contemporary systems of psychology. From one point of view it is correct to say that the entire purpose of Masonic Labour is to bring this indwelling Divine Spark into consciousness.

Figure 4 is a picture of the four worlds which we considered earlier and we can use it to relate the structure of our Temple to our model of the cosmos. The diagram pictures the three lower levels of the psychological vehicle; one, the Ground Floor, in intimate relationship with the physical body; the second level, the Middle Chamber, purely psychological in nature, and the third level, the Holy of Holies, intimately associated with the Spirit. At the very topmost point of the psyche we see its contact with the Divine World.

This allegorical temple which we have been considering describes the structure of the psyche as it is presented by the formulators of the Craft's Symbolism; and we have seen how it corresponds, in a general way with contemporary Jungian concepts. Thus far, however, the structural picture we have drawn lacks vitality; it does not include the consciousness of the individual. That consciousness, and the various degrees of awareness which it can achieve, is represented by the Officers of the Lodge, to whom we will now give our attention.

Consciousness – The Officers of the Lodge

As the Lodge and its accoutrements represent the structure of the psyche, so the seven officers which serve within the Lodge represent seven stages

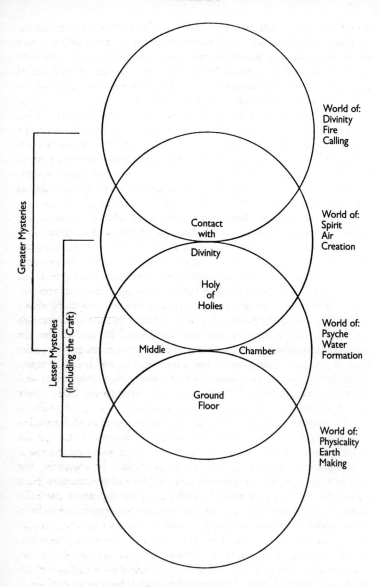

Figure 4

of psychological consciousness possible to the incarnate human being. Although it is customary and correct to think of these officers as a hierarchy, with some having control over others, we must remember also that no officer is more important than another; each stage of consciousness must be functioning and in the correct relationship to the others, if the incarnate individual is to realise his potential.

The first, and most junior, of the officers is the Outer Guard or Tyler. He stands outside the Lodge where he represents that part of the psyche which is in direct contact with the body through the central nervous system and with the physical world through the sense organs. In everyday living we have very little awareness of this body consciousness. Unless the body itself malfunctions through disease, accident or deprivation; or unless we direct our attention to it specifically, it operates pretty much on its own. While a few of its functions, such as breathing, can be controlled consciously within certain limits, the more complex of the essential functions, such as digestion and heartbeat, are usually quite inaccessible and are regulated automatically. Although the physical body is capable of more or less independent operation, it does have real and legitimate demands such as hunger, thirst, sexual drives, appropriate environment, etc. and these demands together with information about the physical world are communicated by the body to the psyche through the level of consciousness represented by the Tyler. We can see that the physical body provides a substantial input of energy to the psyche in the form of physical demands and sensory information, and the Tyler represents that psychological function which first receives this energy and directs it properly. Some of this energy is passed to the more senior officers – higher conscious states of the psyche – as sensory data about the environment and the body itself. A significant part of the incoming energy is passed directly into the unconscious parts of the psyche without the individual being aware of it. Some of this information is used by the autonomic nervous system in its task of regulating the body's functioning. The rest passes into the personal unconscious. Here we see two points which need our attention. First, we can see the Tyler in his role as a guardian, because he protects the consciousness from being swamped by an overload of sensory input from the physical world. Second, we can see why the Tyler must be under conscious control. Many people misuse the Tyler's ability to bypass information to the unconscious to enable them to ignore unpleasant things they do not wish to acknowledge. The phenomenon of being unaware of significant events which occur in one's presence is not an uncommon one.

As we have seen, Freud recognised that the psyche receives a large input from the body. He referred to that part of the unconscious in which this energy originates as the id (although he did not associate the id specifically with the body) and he saw this energy as being associated with constructive and destructive instincts. Freudian psychologists refer to this positive and negative instinctual energy as Libido and Mortido respectively. We will see how the Craft's symbolism deals with this concept of active and passive energy in due course. For the moment we should recognise that the psyche receives a substantial amount of positive and negative energy from the body and its instincts. It will be useful to think of this area from which the body's energy enters the psyche as the sub-conscious and to reserve the term unconscious for the higher stages of awareness within the Temple. The Tyler, as the lowest and most outwardly orientated of the Officers, represents that very important faculty which relates the psyche to its physical vehicle and through it to the physical world.

The second officer in rank and stage of awareness is the Inner Guard. His position within the door indicates that this stage of consciousness is genuinely within the psyche, while his intimate relationship with the Outer Guard indicates that he is very much concerned with the physical world. In the terminology of modern psychology, the Inner Guard represents the ordinary consciousness; the ego. (The word ego is used here in the general context assigned by contemporary psychologists whose models we are using as a framework to study the Craft and whose terminology is in general use. Some nineteenth- and early twentieth-century writers have used the term Ego (capitalised) to represent the interior essence of the individual, a concept which we will identify in this book by the Jungian term, Self). Now, most people give primary attention to the physical world; and in a person so orientated, the ego is directed outward towards the body and its physical activities. The Freudian school of psychology, whose theories were formulated on the basis of observation of people with this orientation, considers the ego to be the executive agency of the individual. Here we see one of the principal differences between the Craft's concept of the human being and that of the Freudian psychologist. If we were to attempt to express the Freudian model in Masonic symbolism, the Inner Guard – the ego – stands in the doorway of the Lodge peering over the Tyler's shoulder, so to speak, and trying as best he can to direct the activity of the body; all the while he is oblivious of the activities of the Lodge which occur behind him in his unconscious. This is an unfortunate situation, because the ego, while a good servant, and routine operator, does not have the capacity or scope of understanding to be a good master. Indeed, it frequently leads the individual into trouble. This is, of course, the situation in which most people find themselves, and it accounts for much human grief – but it falls far short of human potential.

The open lodge is a model of the psyche when it is awake to its potential. In the Masonic model we see that the Inner Guard looks in two directions – inward, to the Junior Warden, to receive instruction from deep within the psyche, and outward to receive perceptions from the body. Here we see the ego operating as it should, as a level of consciousness which mediates between the psyche and the physical world. In this capacity as an intermediary, the Inner Guard, or ego, presents itself in various ways to the world at large. These personae change as the individual finds himself in different situations and this conveys part of the meaning of the Inner Guard's protective role, because the ego usually presents the socially acceptable persona and the world sees only that aspect of the psyche which the Inner Guard/ego presents at the door. Like most sentinals, the Inner Guard functions very nicely in routine situations; and the ego which he represents is properly charged with the supervision of the minute-to-minute routine activities of thinking, doing and feeling in the everyday physical experience. In cases of emergency, however, and in the Open Lodge, which is concerned with serious work at the psychological level, the ego is seen in his proper perspective: as an excellent doorkeeper.

The Deacons are messengers (the title derives from the Greek 'dai-konos' – he who has been pushed through). As states of consciousness, these stages exist, for most people, at or just beyond the threshold of ordinary awareness and they carry 'messages' or reflect the situation from the deeper levels of the psyche (the Principal Officers) to the ego (the Inner Guard). Almost everyone is aware, at some time or another, of the states of consciousness represented by the Deacons which, in contemporary terms, we might call a feeling or intuition and awakening.

The Junior Deacon represents the stage of feeling, intuition or sensitivity which almost everyone recognises from time to time, although some people are far more aware of their intuition than others. Intuition is not directly connected with the physical world, although, of course, it can be related to physical things. Intuition is a sort of direct knowledge which is presented to the Inner Guard (ego) from the Principal Officers deep in the unconscious, together with the reciprocal (and automatic) function of passing external information back to the Principal Officers. One of the most common experiences of the Junior Deacon's message is the pang of conscience. Often we hear a person say, 'I know I have done the wrong thing', even in the absence of external evidence. This sort of message originates quite deep in the psyche (with the Senior Warden, as we shall see) and it is brought to the Inner Guard's (ego's) attention by the Junior Deacon as the intuitive knowledge of the error (or rightness) of one's action. Another frequently recognised example of the Junior Deacon's stage of awareness is the foreboding which warns of a dangerous or unpleasant situation. In films this state is indicated by dark lighting and sinister music, but in real life perceptive people can sense directly the hostility which may be present in an ostensibly congenial surrounding. The intuitions of the Junior Deacon may be responses to external events, or indications of activities in the unconscious; but they, themselves, are relatively superficial in the same way that the message is usually unimportant compared to the event to which it refers.

The Senior Deacon corresponds to the stage of awakening. It is a stage of awareness which is not particularly common in ordinary experience and to attain it confers substantial advantage. To be awake is to be present in the moment. Good athletes experience this sort of awareness immediately prior to a contest. So, also, do lovers when they recognise their relationship and discover their mutual world for the first time. So, too, does the driver of an automobile frequently 'awaken' when his car starts to skid into danger on a slick patch of road. These are situations in which the individuals have been thrust into the awakening stage by external events. Anyone who commutes in a major city can identify easily the stage of awakening. For example, when riding the London Underground, one can 'awaken' and realise suddenly that one has been following automatically a familiar, although quite complex, route through several tube stations, catching the proper trains without conscious attention and without the ability to recall doing so. This habitual behaviour is being asleep, and a large proportion of people live most of their lives in this fashion and complain vociferously when asked to break the pattern. Contrast this habitual behaviour with the state of mind adopted by the infrequent visitor to London who must travel on the Underground changing at two complex stations to arrive at a tightly scheduled appointment. Such a person is awake voluntarily. This state of awakening is characterised by sharpness of image, by an objectivity, by a clarity of perception and by a general alertness to events (both internal and external) and to their implications. Everyone has a few moments of being awake in this sense, and those experiences are generally available as vivid memories because the individual was alert and acutely aware at the time.

A relatively small proportion of people are 'awake' most of the time although their attention is often directed principally outward, toward the world, rather than inward toward their own natures. Such people are alert to the circumstances around them, and because they are awake, they see and seize opportunities of which others are entirely unaware. Thus, they rise to prominence as the leaders in politics, business, trade unions and academe. They are perceived (correctly) as being people of great ability and they manage the affairs of the world, for good or for ill, according to the disposition of the other components of their psyches. When a person commits himself to some sort of programme of self-knowledge, such as the Work of the Craft, the experience of being awake, of being in the place of the Senior Deacon, becomes less uncommon; and in time it becomes a more and more familiar state of mind as one tries to adopt it regularly. The thing which sets the Craftsman apart is that as well as being awake to his external circumstances, he also seeks to be awake to his motives, to the long-term effects of his actions on himself and others, to the personal interior growth he should be trying to achieve, and, not least, to what he can grasp of the intention of Divinity for him (his purpose in the world). Providence frequently offers a moment of awakening by way of encouragement to a person newly started in interior work, and it is usually an ecstatic experience as one sees the symbolic structure of his chosen discipline come to life with great clarity. The ecstasy usually fades, however; the honeymoon period ends, and the hard work, symbolised by Masonic Labour, begins. Gradually one who commits himself to that labour finds that he becomes awake more and more frequently. In this state, the person working on himself is aware, not simply of the situation in the world about him, but of the situation within himself.

The four Officers which we have considered thus far are the Assistant Officers, those whose places and duties are on the floor of the Lodge, the Ground Floor of the Temple. In other words the Assistant Officers all represent levels of consciousness which are concerned in some way with the relationship between the psyche and the body. This situation is reflected in Figure 5. We have seen this diagram before, but now the positions of the Officers are indicated. The Assistant Officers are all to

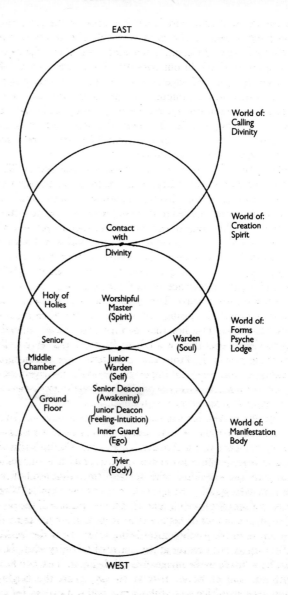

Figure 5

be found on the Ground Floor, the area of the psychological world which interpenetrates the physical world. The situation of the Principal Officers is quite different. Their places are above the floor, and their positions are fixed. In our consideration of these three Officers, who together 'govern the Lodge', it is particularly important to recognise the limitations which are imposed by the nature of ritual. While the three officers are, of necessity, represented symbolically by three separate people, we must remember that the levels of consciousness they represent are not really separate things; they are, rather, three enduring aspects of the individual himself.

The least of these Principal Officers is the Junior Warden. He is associated with the First Degree, the custodian of the Apprentice's tools, and the director of activity on the Ground Floor of the Temple. When this symbolism is applied to the individual, we see the Junior Warden as representing that stage of consciousness which directs – or should direct – the activities of the individual in the physical world. Here is one of the important differences between eastern and western traditions. Many people who are working to develop their interior capacities tend to minimise the importance of ordinary mundane activities; this is an essentially eastern view. The western mind, however, tends to be by nature relatively inquiring and analytical and often requires a way of working which matches that quality. The Craft is such a way; it acknowledges that there is a Divine Plan and that each individual's life has some role in it. From that perspective the circumstance of one's incarnation has some real importance, and the management of one's life in the world is seen as an essential part of one's interior growth in which the Junior Warden plays a central role.

The Junior Warden stands in an important position. In the diagram of the four worlds we have seen each world as a successively grosser reflection of the world above it. The Junior Warden's situation is at the place where the three lower worlds meet, and it is this unique location that gives the individual who operates from that level of consciousness his particular quality. Being at the apex of the Physical World, he is the directing agency of the Ground Floor, the epitome of the physical nature of man, the master of his material situation. At the same time he is at the centre of his psychological being where he is the 'reflection of the reflection' of the Creator at the centre of Divinity; thus, he is reminded that he is 'made in the image of God'. Being in the south he is associated with the sun at noon, that is to say, with the bright unclouded consciousness which sees with clarity, and is aware of his psychological state and the effect it has on people and things around him. His position also touches the bottom of the world of the Spirit which gives him a glimpse of his destiny. This is a stage of consciousness not universally recognised by contemporary psychology. Freud did not incorporate the concept into his theory; but something similar is found in Jung's model as the archetype he calls the Self, the essence of the individual. The location at the junction of the three lower worlds is what gives the Junior Warden/Self its scope and its capacity to integrate the other elements of the psyche. When a person operates from this stage of consciousness he sees his psychological processes and understands his motives clearly. He negotiates with the physical world through his ego which assumes its appropriate role as an intermediary. (This command relationship between Junior Warden and Inner Guard is touched on in the Ceremony of Opening the Lodge and we will examine it in a little detail when we speak of Labour in the First Degree.) At the same time, he can be open to the influence of the Spirit which enlivens him from above.

The Junior Warden is the first glimpse we have of the psyche itself, of that part of the human being which existed before birth and will survive after the body dies. The Senior Warden presides over the Middle Chamber, which associates him with the Second Degree. He represents a stage of consciousness yet more profound than that of his Junior colleague; the Senior Warden symbolises the consciousness of the Soul. Even a cursory review of the Fellowcraft's Working Tools and the Perfect Ashlar of which the Senior Warden is the custodian indicate that the activities which occur in the Soul or Middle Chamber have to do with morality, with trying and testing and with proving against absolute criteria. Consciousness at the stage of the Senior Warden (the Soul) is consciousness of morality; and with this stage of awareness one prescribes the rules by which the Junior Warden (the Self) conducts his business. The Senior Warden (Soul) does not, usually, have much difficulty communicating with the Junior Warden (Self); but in the common situation of an individual working from his ego, his limited consciousness is unaware of the general functioning of his psyche. In such a case the Senior Warden frequently finds it hard to get his message through to consciousness. In this situation the Senior Warden's messenger – the Junior Deacon (intuition) – makes his way to the Inner Guard (ego) and the individual becomes aware of his Soul's activity as a pang of conscience. In the diagram of the Four Worlds (Figure 5) the Senior Warden/Soul is shown occupying the small zone entirely with the psyche, and it is this position that gives the Soul its particular quality. As we have seen, the Ground Floor is in contact with the physical world and the Junior Warden is constrained not only by the laws which operate in the psyche, but also by the physical laws as he conducts his activities. The Worshipful Master is similarly constrained by the laws operating in the spiritual world with which he is intimately associated. But the Senior Warden, the Soul, exists entirely within the psyche and is subject only to the laws of the psychological world. It is in this relative freedom that free will is possible to the human being, and it is the reason morality is the central issue in the Second Degree.

The Worshipful Master serves at the Porchway entrance to the Holy of Holies. This area of the psyche, as the diagram of the Four Worlds (Figure 5) shows, is intimately related to the spiritual world in the same way that the Ground Floor is related to the physical world – at the top it touches the very lowest part of Divinity. As the Junior Warden is the Manager who integrates the psyche and oversees the work and the Senior Warden is the Controller who sets the standards, so the Worshipful Master is the Director who establishes the objectives and defines the policies. He is qualified to do so because, at this level of consciousness one sees past one's personal considerations to perceive the needs and aspirations of one's tribe, one's nation or perhaps of the race as a whole. It is a difficult state of consciousness to comprehend, relating as it does to the Third Degree, 'to a complete understanding (of which) few attain'. We will examine the Worshipful Master in a little greater detail when we consider the Master Mason's Degree. For the moment we should recognise that from this position one can 'touch the hem of the Robe'; and one can come, if it be the Divine Will, into the presence of the Most High.

Here then, is the Craft's model of the human psyche, a three-storey temple for indwelling Divinity in which seven Officers serve. The latter represent seven stages of consciousness which range from awareness of physicality at the bottom, to contact with Divinity at the top. The psyche is by no means a static environment. It is, rather, an area of intense activity. We will complete our preliminary overview of the Craft's model by considering the laws which govern this psychological activity.

Dynamics – The Basic Laws

The Tracing Board of the First Degree, which is shown in one of its most popular forms in Figure 6, is a remarkable drawing which depicts two

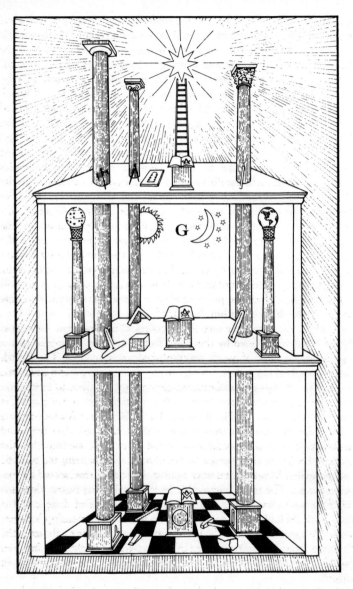

Figure 6

quite different objects. The first is a representation of the psychological world to which we were introduced in our discussion of the geometric progression in Chapter 1. This part of the picture is composed of the Glory, Heavens, Columns and Chequered Pavement, together with the various tools and other implements. These, as we shall observe shortly, reflect the four levels of the psychological world, and the laws by which the psyche operates. The second object which is represented on the board is the individual human being. He consists, diagramatically, of the Point-within-a-circle-bounded-by-two-parallel-lines, the Ladder, and the Glory. Both objects are built on the same plan, the structure of the Divine World, the Image of God. Thus, there are three principles running through each; the Pillars in the general picture correspond to the Parallel Lines and the Ladder in the individual. There are four levels in each, the three principal rungs of the Ladder define the individual's consciousness in terms of three levels which are paralleled by the Pavement, Columns and Heavens in the larger picture. Both the individual and the psychological world share the Divine Glory as their common source. There is a great deal of information to be had from the contemplation of the Board and this dual picture it presents, but we will consider it here from the point of view of understanding the dynamic processes which occur within the psyche.

Our first glimpse of the sort of psychological development envisioned by the Craft is provided by the Three Immovable Jewels, which give a clue as to the sort of work accomplished at each level. The Rough Ashlar, a building stone fresh from the quarry, represents the Apprentice. It rests on the Chequered Pavement, the Ground Floor, and the ritual tells us that smoothing it, that is refining the lower psyche, is the Apprentice's work. The diagram shows the Perfect Ashlar hanging from a Lewis which elevates it above the Chequered Pavement and associates it with the middle area of the Board. We are told that the work of the Second Degree has to do, in part, with proving the tools of the individual Mason's character against the criteria represented by this perfect stone. The third Immovable Jewel, the Tracing Board, does not relate to individual stones at all. It is an instrument of design; and it deals with the building as a whole, that is with the relationship between stones. We may infer from the Immovable Jewels that the Labour in the first two Degrees is accomplished by the individual working on his own faculties, while the Work of the Third Degree is trans-personal in nature.

As the candidate proceeds through the Degrees, he finds that he is introduced to this model, which is represented on the Board. The ritual presents it as a Temple that is already in existence, which is a concept of real significance when viewing the Craft as a psychology. Many contemporary psychologists consider the psyche to be a product of activity which occurs in the brain and thus consider that the psyche is built as the individual grows from infancy through childhood to maturity. The alternative view is that the psyche – or more precisely, the soul, the essence of the psyche – exists before this life-time, occupies the body for an appropriate period, and will continue to exist after the body dies. In this latter view – which is reminiscent of Jung's concept of the psyche being a whole system – is the one expressed by the symbol of the Temple already in existence. The psychological development of infancy, childhood and adolescence serves to build only that portion of the psyche which provides the interface between the immortal soul and the physical world. In the course of this development, the individual comes to grips with several basic psychological laws, which the Craft teaches through the use of the First Degree Tracing Board. We will refer to these laws many times throughout the course of this book; and, of course, we have seen them before.

The first and most fundamental law in all the Craft's teaching is concealed in the Ornaments of the Lodge. These are the Mosaic Pavement, the Blazing Star and Indented or Tessellated Border. Jointly and severally, these three objects embody and communicate the Law of Unity. The Blazing Star, or Glory, in the centre of the Board represents that Unity as Divinity, the basis of all the manifest universe and the objective of our labours at this stage. Its presence on the Tracing Board reminds us of the Divine Presence in each of us. The Chequered Pavement represents that same Unity as it is perceived in manifestation at the opposite pole of existence, in the physical world. Here we see Unity represented by seemingly opposing phenomena (black and white) which, none the less, complement one another and fit together with precision into the single entity represented by the pavement. The Tessellated Border, which from an artistic point of view binds the whole thing together, is not around the pavement as we would expect, but around the board as a whole. By this use of the border, the diagram conveys the idea that the entire thing is a Unity, a single, integrated system. This underlying unity has several very significant implications. First, since it is a single system, the same laws operate throughout, governing the most powerful archangel and the least significant human being. This is the basis of the validity of the old saying 'As above, so below', and is the reason why through the study of an individual man one can come to understand all things. The second implication is that in a single, integrated system events do not happen at random. The apparently unconnected events of our everyday experience do actually form a coherent pattern analogous to the Chequered Pavement even though we may only rarely perceive it. In fact, one of our tasks is so to relate and comprehend the events of our experience as to be able to understand this pattern. We will look at this idea again when we examine the concept of fate. For the moment; it is enough to recognise the Law of Unity and to realise that all of existence is 'a garment without a seam'.

The Law of Opposites is shown on the First Degree Tracing Board in a variety of ways. We have already noted the Chequered Pavement which emphasises the complementary aspects of the opposites as well as their inherent oneness through the Law of Unity. A more subtle, but in some ways more useful, representation of the Law of Opposites is found in the figure called a Point-within-a-circle-bounded-by-two-parallel-lines. This is a complex symbol which must be interpreted in the context of the entire central part of the Board. We will look at it in detail later, but here we should note that the parallel lines represent the Law of Opposites. These lines are said to represent Moses and Solomon; Moses the Prophet, who received the revelation of God, and Solomon the King, who administered the Law of God, are a traditional Jewish representation of paired opposites. In some forms of the ritual, the parallel lines are related to the Saints John. Since the Feast of the Baptist is Midsummer and that of the Evangelist is Midwinter, the image of the Law of Opposites is quite clear. The Wardens' Columns, which are akin to the parallel lines, also allude to the Law of Opposites, in as much as the solid stability of Strength and the exuberant vitality of Beauty tend to complement each other. These symbols, like the Pavement, point to the fact that in the relative universe in which we live, we experience Divinity as complementary (sometimes seemingly opposed) pairs. But while the Pavement stresses the fundamental unity of the pairs, the Parallel Lines and the Wardens' Columns introduce us to a different idea. Both the Lines and the Columns as we have considered them here are each part of a more complex symbol. The Lines must also be interpreted in the context of the point, the circle and the Ladder; and the Wardens' Columns must also be understood together with a third element, the Master's Column. In this way the Law of Opposites leads us directly to the Rule of Three.

The Lodge is said to be supported by three Pillars, denominated Wisdom, Strength and Beauty. They are among the most prominent features on the Tracing Board and in our picture of the three-storey Temple (Figure 3) these Pillars extend through all three levels. They embody the Law known in old Masonic writings as the Rule of Three, or, as we might call it in modern jargon, 'Three Agency Dynamic Stability'. The Rule of Three states that stability can be achieved and maintained by the action of two opposing agencies which are held in balance by the mediation of a third agency which acts between the two. One can easily observe the Rule of Three at work in a crude way by considering a house with central heating. In this example the effects of a heat-producing furnace (active agency) and a heat-absorbing winter environment (passive agency) are held in dynamic equilibrium by a thermostat (the mediating agency) to produce a comfortable environment. More subtly, but still on the physical level, the metabolism of the human body co-ordinates the anabolic processes – which absorb energy to build tissue – and katabolic processes – which break down tissue to release energy – to maintain normal body weight and functions. More generally and from the psychological point of view the Rule of Three states that energy is distributed around the psyche in such a way that the psyche as a whole (conscious and unconscious) is held in balance. The controlling or mediating agency may be conscious or unconscious but it operates in either case.

In our model of the psyche, these three agencies take the names given to the three pillars – the active, outpouring quality of Beauty; the steady, containing quality of Strength; and the observant, compassionate co-ordination of Wisdom. These principles are sometimes called Mercy, Severity and Clemency; or Day, Night and Divine Will. The active pillar of Beauty can be thought of as containing all the instincts and urges to live which Freud called Libido, while the passive pillar of Strength contains the instincts to repress and destroy which the Freudians refer to as Mortido. In the most mature situation, we can recognise the co-ordinating agency to be consciousness. This concept of interaction between three agencies contains the ideas of compensation, opposition and synthesis among elements of the psyche which we saw in our consideration of Jung's concepts of psychodynamics. We will spend more time considering this law, in one form or another, than any of the others. As we have said, it always operates, and when it operates without our conscious control it can work to our detriment, as we shall see. The Rule of Three forms the basis of most Masonic Labour; and we will come to realise how loudly our ancient brethren spoke when they said: 'He who would a Master be, must observe the Rule of Three.'

The Law of Four Levels has to do with structure. We saw in our review of cosmology that there were four levels in the Divine World of Adam Kadmon. Since the Universe is said to reflect Divinity, the levels give rise to the four worlds shown in Figures 4 and 5: since each world is conceived as a reflection of the Divine World, each world has these levels; and the four levels of the psychological world are shown clearly on the First Degree Tracing Board.

The Chequered Pavement corresponds to the Ground Floor, and represents that part of the psyche which is in contact with the body and the physical world. This is the Level of Action and can be equated (in ordinary experience) with Jung's concept of individual consciousness.

The Central Area, including the Altar, Great Lights and Three Columns, corresponds to the Middle Chamber and represents the Soul. This is the area which lies exclusively within the psyche in Figure 5. It is the level of Emotion and equates in a general way with Jung's concept of personal unconscious.

The top of the Board, depicting the Heavens, corresponds to the Holy of Holies and represents that area deep in the psyche which is in contact with the World of Spirit. This is the Level of Intellect and can be thought of as similar to Jung's concept of the collective unconscious.

The Blazing Star, or Glory, in the centre of the Board is symbolic of the Divine Presence which resides in the Holy of Holies.

We can see immediately that these levels reflect the four levels to be found in the Divine World. In this way the Craft teaches the concept that both man and the relative universe are made in the Image of God. This structure also provides the form of the Craft's model of psychological development, since the participation in the Three Degrees implies conscious experience at each level.

The last of the Laws we will consider might be called the Law of Increasing Complexity. As one progresses downward from the Divine World, farther from the source, one becomes subject to a more stringent law. We can observe this illustrated in a variety of ways in the Craft. On the Tracing Board, the Divine Presence, the Glory, is only itself; the Heavens have three elements – the sun, moon and stars. At the Middle Level, the Board begins to look complicated with the Columns, Altar, Great Lights, etc. while the Floor seems almost cluttered with a variety of symbols. In a similar way, the Three Lodges have a progressively smaller minimum complement – 7, 5 and 3 as one enters progressively higher degrees. An understanding of this principle should prepare the candidate in Freemasonry for an experience of greater freedom as he progresses in the work. At the same time it should warn him that although he has greater freedom, he is not above the law, simply that at higher levels of consciousness, the laws operate with less stringency and permit the individual greater latitude in his behaviour.

The First Degree Tracing Board also defines a dimension to which reference is made throughout the ritual. It is the East-West direction. With East at the top of the Board, the direction of the Heavens and the Glory, and West at the bottom, next to the chequered floor of the physical world, the Board describes East-West as a continuum which we can understand to be the 'Dimension of Consciousness'. We have already seen this dimension in Figure 5 where we placed the East at the top, in the World of Divinity, and West at the bottom, in the physical world. For the moment, we will content ourselves with noting this dimension as the Tracing Board defines it. We will see this again in the Second Degree.

The reader will certainly realise that he has seen these laws before. They are those we observed in connection with the Divine World of Azilut when we looked at the cosmology which underlies the Craft's symbolism. In this way the Craft communicates two notions: First, that mankind is 'made in the image of God', and second, that he reflects, in miniature, the structure of the universe. This correspondence between the Universe, the macrocosm, and man, the microcosm, is the basis of the instruction 'Man, know thyself, and thou shall know God' which is the principle upon which the Craft and most western systems of interior development is based.

Of the basic laws which have been outlined above, we must be particularly careful to remember the Law of Unity. Caught up in all the detail of Craft symbolism, it is easy to forget it; but it is the law which holds the entire system together. Ultimately, each candidate is required to demonstrate his understanding of it. That demonstration is for the experienced Craftsman, however, and much labour precedes it.

To accomplish that labour is to accomplish one's own psychological development by bringing the principles we have discussed above into conscious experience. As the Craft's ritual indicates, it is a progressive business which starts with the work of the Apprentice on the Ground Floor of the Temple. It is to the Ground Floor, and the psychological work accomplished there, that we now turn our attention.

CHAPTER 3
The Ground Floor

1 THE CEREMONY OF INITIATION

The new Freemason is introduced to the symbolic structure we have been discussing by participating as a candidate in the ceremonies of the Three Degrees. The degrees themselves represent discrete events in each of which the consciousness of the candidate is seen to expand to embrace a new level in the Temple of the psyche. Although those events actually occur in the experience of one who pursues the Masonic Tradition in the way we are examining it here, they do not usually occur at the time the Degrees are conferred. Indeed, the Craft's symbolism seems to be designed in such a way that the entire system is first introduced in its symbolic form over a brief period. Then the individual Mason who chooses to do so works through the Degrees again, this time actually in the process of living. During this latter process, which may require an entire lifetime, the ceremonies of the Degrees provide references and explanation for the actual experiences of the individual. As we look at these ceremonies, we will not follow the candidate's progress in a descriptive manner. We will, instead, comment on certain salient features to put the events into the perspective from which the book is working.

Before the candidate is admitted to the Lodge to participate in the Ceremony of his Initiation he is 'properly prepared'. The Junior Deacon attends to the preparation; and from that officer's role as the Senior Warden's messenger we may infer that, in one's actual experience, preparation for the start of interior work is a process which is conducted by the Soul and is brought into consciousness by the individual's intuition. In practice (contrasted to ceremony) the preparation is likely to be a lengthy process and one of which the individual is likely to be only partially aware. Everyone has had a moment which indicates that there is 'something more'. It may be a brief conversation at a party, a book which catches one's eye on a bookstall, a comment dropped by a business associate, or any similar event; but the quality is that the experience triggers a response deep inside. If one recognises the response, ponders on it, and follows up on the subject, then the process of preparation begins. In the course of one's normal activity more related material turns up. A new idea comes from a discussion with a friend and is incorporated into one's view of the world, perhaps replacing an old concept which is then discarded. A fragment of an idea is picked up from a newspaper article, a new interpretation emerges from the text of a familiar book. Unlikely agencies contribute to this process quite unwittingly. For example, a business trip or a posting in connection with the Armed Forces may serve to bring the alert individual into contact with the person or idea he needs next. Slowly, perhaps over a period of several years, one's concepts change, one's frame of reference is modified until he can accommodate directly the concepts which are associated with the Work. This is the process of 'proper preparation' in its actual (contrasted to symbolic) form. When it is complete, when the prospective candidate's heart is open and he is receptive, he knocks (in the Masonic idiom) on the door of his Lodge, that is, at the entrance to his interior self.

The Ceremony of Initiation, which is the candidate's introduction to the Craft and its symbolism, is said to take place on the Ground Floor of the Temple. We have seen that this level corresponds to that part of the psyche which is directly related to the physical world. It is the part of the psyche immediately beyond the threshold of consciousness, represented by the Door of the Lodge; and the candidate himself initiates the Ceremony by knocking on the Door. The candidate should give these knocks himself. In general, he knocks incorrectly, and learns that one does not gain access to a Masonic Lodge except by the 'proper knocks'. But instructions on how to knock properly are provided from the Worshipful Master. In a sense, this instruction which enables the candidate to gain admission is the final step in the lengthy process of preparation which has been carefully managed by the Soul from deep within the candidate's own being. At last, he gives the proper knocks for himself. The knocks, together with the passages in the ritual which recapitulate the prerequisites and motivations appropriate for membership, serve to remind him that is something he is doing of his own volition and for himself. It is not being done to him, nor is he doing it as a favour for another.

Early in the ceremony, the Lodge offers a prayer for the benefit of the candidate. It is the first of many prayers and serves to introduce a fundamental requirement into the instruction. The prayer itself points out that dedication to the Deity – as the candidate defines It – is the means by which one becomes successful as a member of the Craft. The candidate's affirmation of his trust in the Deity is also required at this time. Here, since it is one of the few places where the candidate must speak for himself, one finds that in an actual ceremony he is sometimes prompted by the Deacon so that the ceremony shall proceed smoothly. While prompting may seem to be reasonable from the point of view of good ritual, it is quite improper from our point of view. No one who needs the prompt, who is unsure of his trust in Deity, should undertake Masonic Labour in the sense that we are considering it here. The psyche is the Watery World. Like the sea itself, it is a potentially hazardous environment with currents, tides, rocks and shoals. In places it is devoid of landmarks and reference points. Faith in the Deity is a reference (analogous to the mariner's compass) which will provide direction when other sources fail. As strangely as the idea may fall on twentieth-century western ears, no one should undertake to explore the psyche without placing his trust in the Deity.

By the manner of his reception, the candidate is made aware of two dangers, which he will not understand for some time. The dangers associated with rashness and reticence are such that to avoid one is to increase the risk of the other. It is the lesson of Charybdis and Scylla, and the symbol provides instructions on the attitude appropriate for one about to undertake interior work. He must proceed slowly, steadily and carefully with the work in hand, even when it is boring, and he must avoid rushing hastily into new and unfamiliar situations, no matter how attractive. The need for this sort of balance between action and stillness will characterise the new Mason's entire career, and we will return to the concept in one form or another again and again. The candidate is asked, as we have already seen, to persevere through the ceremony. Resolute but cautious perseverance is the required frame of mind. Every candidate agrees without second thought to the ritual's questions about motive and perseverance; but one who would really embark on interior work should review the two dangers and the questions about motive and perseverance with care. This is the last chance to abandon the undertaking without serious detriment.

Although the term is not used during the ceremony, the Entered Apprentice Freemason is represented in the Craft's symbolism as a Rough Ashlar, or building stone. In the complete symbol, the body of humanity is represented as a quarry from which stone is to be cut to construct a temple to Deity. Ultimately, all of the rock in the quarry is to be incorporated in the building. While the rock remains in the quarry, it is part of the mass and it experiences what the mass experiences. The candidate in the Entered Apprentice Degree is about to separate himself out, and to undertake to live his life as an individual, to be a separate stone. It is a step which only he can take; and he can take it only for himself. When he has done it, when he has recognised himself to be an individual, like the Rough Ashlar cut from the mountain which will never be part of the bedrock again, the Entered Apprentice can never go back. To put it another way, when one has had an insight in to his nature, when he has a glimpse of the fact that he really is, inside, at the core of his being the 'Image of God', he can never unknow it. When a person knows what he is, and acknowledges it, he is responsible for himself from that time onward. He will be an individual, with individual responsibility for the rest of his life.

The candidate's status as an Entered Apprentice is confirmed by his obligation. The Craft does not ask much of an Entered Apprentice. His obligation requires only that he keep the secrets of the Order, and this subject deserves a little attention. People who observe Freemasonry from outside the Order, and particularly from outside the perspective we are using in this book, regard it as a physical organisation in the physical world. In the physical world secrecy is associated with security and with concealment, and those with this orientation find it easy to believe that any secret must conceal some sinister activity or at least some activity of which one is ashamed. In this ordinary sense of the word, there is virtually nothing in Freemasonry to be kept secret. In any case, the overwhelming preponderance of the symbolic structure, ritual and writing is defined by the United Grand Lodge of England as being 'intensely personal', but not secret. Only the means by which Masons recognise one another are said to be secret, and even those few 'secrets' have been compromised frequently by apostates. Indeed, there are some six million Masons in the world; and it is difficult to argue that anything known to six million people is a secret in any ordinary sense of the word.

The perspective we are using here, however, does not consider Masonry as a physical organisation, but as a God-centred psychology. In the psychological world, secrecy is not a simple device for security – secrecy is a container. Anyone who is involved in the creative process, or who knows someone who is, will recognise this function of secrecy immediately. Creative artists regularly apply this principle by containing their work, holding it close until it is ready to be manifested. Such people have learned by experience that a failure to contain their work drains off their energy and destroys their creativity. It is in this context that we should understand the obligation for secrecy imposed on the Entered Apprentice. As he works with the principles of the Craft, he will learn about the nature of himself and his relationship to the universe and to Divinity. These are intensely personal experiences and secrecy is the container within which the individual preserves them. It is this criticially important interior process which the Craft nurtures by the use of its external symbol of secrecy.

In the past, the candidate was required to agree to his obligation under the constraint of a severe penalty. The penalties in the Craft appear, at first glance, to be quite horrific and quite out of place in an otherwise benign organisation; and they are no longer required of the candidate for that reason. His attention is still drawn to them, however, and that is a measure of their importance. A little quiet reflection on the penalties will reveal that they were never intended to be imposed as a punishment. They are, rather, a serious warning to the candidate, and they are carefully devised, singularly appropriate and absolutely necessary. The need for the penalties derives from the fact that as one learns more and more about one's self, one develops greater capabilities, assumes greater responsibilities and incurs greater risk. The Working Tools of each degree make reference to the capabilities, which are also called 'inestimable privileges'. The obligations outline the responsibilities. The penalties define the risks. The key to understanding the penalties correctly is to remember two things. First, that the Craft is a type of psychology and the penalties, while set in physical terms, in fact, describe psychological phenomena. Second, that the penalties are not something which might be done to the individual by the Craft, should he violate his obligation. Rather, they are the inevitable result of the normal operation of psychological processes initiated by a certain type of behaviour – that sort of behaviour which is prohibited by the obligation. In this context, the penalties serve as good and timely warnings. The nature of each penalty is representative of the particular psychological difficulty which departure from the obligation is likely to cause. In the case of the Entered Apprentice, indiscriminate discussion of his newly found interior life will result in his severing his internal connection with his source as well as being stuck in a sterile environment – a salty place between the 'earthy' physical world and the 'watery' psychological world – in which no growth is possible.

With his obligation complete, the candidate is restored to light to symbolise that, having recognised his individuality and accepted the responsibility that goes with it, he is able to see in a limited way into the workings of the psyche. The first things he sees are the Three Great, but emblematic, Lights. Their location in the Lodge indicates that the reality they represent exists deep within the psyche of the individual. Actually, the Three Great Lights and the candidate who contemplates them form a composite representation of Man as a miniature of the Universe as it is represented in Figure 5. The candidate's body represents the physical world as well as his own physical nature. The Square, the instrument concerned with form, represents the psychological world (the World of Formation) as well as the individual's psychological nature. The Compasses represent the Spiritual World and the individual's Spiritual Being, while the Volume of Sacred Law represents the World of Divinity and the contact with that Divine Source. In each Degree the arrangement of these Great Lights reflects the depth of awareness which characterises the individual who has reached that level. The particular configuration of these symbols in the First Degree indicates that the Entered Apprentice is conscious primarily at the level of his psychological nature. Whenever they appear together, however, the arrangement of these implements always emphasises the fact that mankind, and the entire universe, has its source in Divinity.

At this time, after he has made his commitment, the newly made Entered Apprentice is given the signs by which he will identify himself as a Mason. These are, officially, the Masonic secrets. From the point of view we are considering, however, the signs too, are allegorical and are representative of a reality far more subtle than a physical mode of recognition. We can get something of a feeling for the real nature of 'signs' by examining a situation which is reasonably common in ordinary experience and not directly related to the Craft. There is a quality possessed by men and women who have experienced serious crises and coped with them successfully. People who have this quality recognise it immediately in others; those who do not have this quality are entirely oblivious to it. This quality is a 'sign' in the sense that we are trying to understand the term. It identifies the person who exhibits it as a particular sort of person; one who can cope with crisis. The 'sign' of an Entered Apprentice, understood from this point of view is that quality which he exhibits which marks him as one who has assumed responsibility for himself and his actions. He may not be very good at handling that responsibility, at least at first; but that is the quality which will be his identifying characteristic during the years he spends as an Entered Apprentice.

The Senior Warden entrusts the candidate with the Distinguishing Badge of a Mason. It is the most familiar of Masonic emblems and is, of course, widely used within the Craft to proclaim a Brother's Masonic Rank. As a symbol in the context that we are developing, the badge sets out a relatively complex idea. In Figure 5, we have set out the doctrine of the four worlds and seen that the human being has the capacity – and ultimately the responsibility – to work in all four. To accomplish this task, he has a vehicle or body appropriate to each of these worlds. The physical body, with which we are all familiar, is the vehicle for operating in the physical world; the Badge is a representation of the vehicle appropriate for operating in the psychological world. We should note that it is the Senior Warden who entrusts the Badge to the candidate. We have seen that the Senior Warden represents the individual's soul. As it is the soul which enclothes the Spirit of the individual as it makes its journey from the Divine source through the worlds toward incarnation, so the officer who symbolises the soul invests the candidate with the emblem of that ethereal garment. The investiture indicates that the candidate's psychological vehicle is starting to develop, while its simplicity and the way it is worn in the Entered Apprentice Degree suggest that at this stage of the individual's development his psychological vehicle is innocent and its various parts are not yet integrated. We will speak in greater detail about the individual's progress through the worlds when we look at the Second Degree.

The new Apprentice starts his labours at the bottom, as the Craft is quick to point out, with its demand for charity. This demand is the foundation stone upon which some of the world's most significant charitable institutions have been built, and genuinely remarkable benefit has resulted from this bit of ritual within and without the Craft. Yet even this has its more subtle implication. The candidate's poverty is not simply monetary, but more fundamentally he is poor in terms of his understanding of himself, in the context of the work of the Craft. Should he, by dint of hard work and Divine Grace, become expert in the Craft, this demand for charity requires that he commit himself to the continuation of the Work. But for the new Entered Apprentice, standing in the north-east corner of the Lodge, that requirement is a long way in the future. Before he can fulfil that obligation, he must come to a knowledge of himself by accomplishing substantial Masonic Labour and for that he requires the detailed instructions provided by the Charge.

2 THE CHARGE TO THE ENTERED APPRENTICE

If the Craft does not demand much in the way of obligations from an Entered Apprentice, neither does it offer him a great deal in terms of rights and privileges. This restricted scope of activity reflects the fact that, in the context of the Craft's model of the psyche, he has access to less than a third of his capacity. He has, in fact, three rights, two of which concern us at the moment. The first right is to attend his Lodge and participate in the Labour of the First Degree. The second right is to receive good instruction. In the ordinary way of things, instruction to an Apprentice consists of simple assistance in learning the brief ritual responses associated with the examination prior to the Second Degree. From our point of view, however, the Craft provides a rich body of instruction with which the newly made Mason can commence the work of coming to know himself. This instruction starts with the Charge to the Entered Apprentice which can be understood as a collection of wise counsels for anyone who is starting to develop his interior capacities.

The Charge opens with a reference to the antiquity of the Order, 'having subsisted from time immemorial'. Superficially, this notion conflicts with the historical evidence which, as we have seen, dates the Craft from the fifteenth or sixteenth centuries. The clue to the correct interpretation is to be found in the use of the word 'subsist' which means literally to 'stand below', to exist at the lowest level. In this context the word conveys the Craft's connection with the central teaching which has always existed just below the level of common awareness. Here, also, the candidate is advised to look at the lowest and most profound level, beneath the surface of the Craft's ritual, to discern its real meaning. With this frame of reference established, the candidate is reminded of the three obligations which are incumbent upon every human being, but which are of particular importance to one who is committed to the Work: these are the duties one owes to God, to one's neighbour and to one's self. In keeping with the Craft's attitudes on the subject, the Charge describes the candidate's duty to God by recommending to him the practice of his own religion, to which the work of the Craft is only secondary. One's duty to one's neighbour is stated in terms of the Golden Rule which, in this case, is more than a statement of conventional morality. It is, rather, a rule of conduct based on the principle of Unity. In a single, integrated system, each action affects the entire structure. In the last analysis, what one does to another one does, in fact, do to one's self; and the farther one progresses in the

Work, the more immediate and apparent does this fact become.

The Craft's notion of one's duty to one's self might be restated in modern terms as, 'keep a sound mind in a sound body'. This may seem strange advice from a discipline which proposes to deal with things beyond the ordinary physical world, and in many respects it is an incomplete statement of duty to one's self. It is the part of wisdom, however; because, as the serious candidate will soon learn, labour on one's self is plain hard work. At times it will require all he can muster in terms of physical and mental stamina.

The charge makes very specific requirements that the person who pursues this interior work shall be a law-abiding citizen in all respects. This requirement for civil obedience applies specifically to that country in which the individual may find himself to be living, as well as to his own country. Now, the Craft is well aware that many governments are oppressive of their citizens; indeed, the Craft itself has suffered from more than a few of such authorities. The purpose of this requirement is not to condone such governments, or even to enjoin good citizenship in general, but to direct the candidate's attention toward his real objectives in the Work. Changes in social institutions may be desirable, in some cases they may be generally welcomed, and people are surely needed to bring about those changes: but that is not the work of the Craft, nor is it, usually, the business of one who has chosen to develop his inner faculties. Indeed, involvements with the plots and intrigues of politics will usually hinder one's personal development and slow his real work, which, if he performs it correctly will be far more effective in bringing harmony into the world than any political undertaking. The reference to 'the allegience due to the Sovereign of your native land' and to the 'indissoluble attachment towards that country' serves as a reminder in this case. One should remember the cosmology that we developed in Chapter 1, Section 3, and consider whence one came, and who that 'Sovereign' is likely to be. In any case, the candidate is reminded that interior development is usually slowed or prevented by intense commitment to the improvement of institutions in the physical world. Interior work makes a very real contribution in that respect, but it usually is a subtle and indirect contribution. The Charge's admonitions on citizenship conclude by recommending the practice of the cardinal virtues of Prudence, Temperance, Fortitude and Justice. These are Platonic ideas (from the *Republic*) where they were said to be essential to a well ordered society. The Craft speaks of them as associated with the Apprentice and they are certainly necessary if one is to enter one's own 'Lodge' and operate it effectively as a well ordered organisation.

In a more specific way, the Charge addresses the behaviour relating to the Work itself, stressing secrecy, fidelity and obedience. These terms have very specific contexts in the Craft's instruction. Secrecy is the first point raised. We have already examined the Craft's reasons for requiring its members to hold their experiences close. The repetition here of an injunction covered so emphatically earlier only serves to underscore the importance of the subject. Like secrecy, fidelity is used in the Charge with a quite specific connotation. It means that in pursuing one's Masonic Labours, that is in learning about oneself, one should stay within the rules and practices set out by the Craft. The Craft comprises an order of instruction in a subject area which is outside ordinary experience – the symbolic structure, constitutions and ancient landmarks, together with the individual's life experiences, comprise the curriculum. Fidelity, as used here, implies that one will pursue the course of instruction and not attempt to alter the symbolism to fit his own preconceptions. The object is to make a change in the candidate, not in the curriculum. The rituals and doctrines prescribed by the Craft are established as they are to make the process of interior growth safe and as easy as possible; they should be observed faithfully for that reason. The prohibition from extorting or improperly obtaining the secrets of a superior degree are particularly worthy of note as a practice of fidelity understood in this way. As our outline of the Craft's model of the psyche indicates, the various Degrees represent progressively higher levels of consciousness. As one grows in the work – symbolised by receiving superior degrees – one sees things from the perspective of these higher levels. Like the period of preparation, advancement to the actual higher degrees of consciousness occurs very gradually as the individual makes himself ready for the new perspectives. Now, there are various exercises and devices for extending ordinary consciousness into these higher levels by more or less artificial means. The so called 'mind-expanding' drugs introduced in the 1960s are only the most recent of these artificial mechanisms which have been forbidden by almost all conscientious western Mystery teachings. All such artificial methods of accelerating the expansion of consciousness have some attendant danger because until one can perceive naturally, one is not prepared to evaluate correctly the perspective from higher levels of awareness. Reports from those who use LSD describe ecstatic experiences which 'blow your mind' or the more horrific material of the 'bad trip'; both represent a view of the upper worlds distorted through the individual's ordinary perceptions of reality. When a person gets an insight into the upper worlds through the process of normal psychological maturation it may be amazing and unexpected, but it is not usually mind-blowing or horrific. More recently developed drugs are said to have a more gentle effect, but the difficulty is the same. Under the influence of such drugs one perceives things differently than when in the normal state, and upon returning from the experience one has no way of knowing that he has evaluated his experience correctly. This sort of extension of consciousness by artificial means is the practice to which the Craft refers when it prohibits one from 'improperly extorting the secrets of a higher degree'. Obedience also has a very particular meaning. The Lodge is ruled by three Principal Officers, to which the members are to practice perfect submission, when they are in the execution of their office, in order to ensure harmony among the Brethren. As we have seen, the Officers who rule the Lodge are representations of principles which govern the operation of the psyche. It is to this internal set of 'Officers' that the demand for obedience most particularly applies. We will spend a great deal of time examining these 'Officers' and considering the implications and result of obedience to them.

Next comes an almost casual reference to the Liberal Arts and Sciences as a curriculum. In fact, these seven subjects comprise a very old course of study for the development of consciousness, and we will examine them in a little more detail when we look at the Second Degree in which they play a more prominent role. Here we might do well to note that the first three – Grammar, the discipline by which verbal communication is actively assembled; Rhetoric, the technique by which communication is infused with feeling; and Logic, the process by which thoughtful analysis is introduced, are those most suited for study by the Apprentice. The process of acting, thinking and feeling will be seen as similar to Jung's functions of sensation, intuition, thinking and feeling. Both represent sets of psychological activities potentially available to the control of the ego, and it is these with which the Apprentice will commence his work.

The Charge closes with the comment that, while a daily advance in the Masonic knowledge is expected, one should not neglect 'the ordinary duties of your station in life'. This is not a reference to the social structure of the sixteenth century, but an insight into the Craft's working method. In the broadest sense there are two approaches to interior development. In the cloistered approach, which appears to be typical of many of the eastern traditions at the present time, one retires from the world, in the fashion of a monk or hermit, and attempts to achieve the highest stages of conscious awareness. The worldly approach requires that one remain in contact with the practices and usages of everyday living, and extract one's lessons from the application of principles to the day to day experiences provided by the worldly environment. Neither approach is superior to the other, rather, each has its specific characteristics which makes it appropriate to specific people in particular circumstances. The worldly approach is more commonly practised in western urban societies where retirement from the world is difficult. Moreover, it appears that it is an approach which is more generally well suited to contemporary western temperament. The Craft states quite clearly in this part of the Charge that it uses this latter working method. In this way it eliminates the excuse (which some might be otherwise tempted to offer) that the problems of day-to-day activities prevent progress; the day-to-day activities and the problems they present are the fabric of the curriculum!

Having assumed responsibility for himself and received this set of rules for his general conduct, the newly made Mason is ready, at last, to begin his study of the symbolic structure which provides an insight into the nature of his psyche and to apply what he learns to his own experience. That is, he is ready for Masonic Labour.

3 THE WORK OF THE ENTERED APPRENTICE

The Command Relationship

In the commonly held view Masonic Labour is considered to be the business of performing the rituals and ceremonies of the Craft. These activities certainly form an essential part of the work called Labour, and when they are done properly they require substantial attention and energy. From our point of view, however, these rituals and ceremonies comprise only the smallest part of a much larger body of activities which make up the labours undertaken by a Mason.

In the broadest and most important sense the purpose of Masonic Labour is to render service to God. In the more immediate sense the objective of Masonic Labour for the new Apprentice is to come to know that his psychological apparatus is in the form represented by the three-storeyed Temple described in the Craft's symbolism. 'Know' is a carefully chosen word; it is not enough to understand that one has a soul, spirit and contact with Divinity; it is not enough even to believe it. The object of Masonic Labour is to know; and knowledge, in this sense, implies direct, individual experience of the thing. Stated in the simplest terms, the Mason working in this way tries to utilise the day-to-day events of his life as an opportunity to see the principles taught by the Craft operating in his experience. He regards his life as a school which presents him with instruction into the nature of himself. This attitude does not imply that everyone should live the same life in an outward sense. Rather, it suggests that, if one will observe, Providence (whose business it is to provide, after all) will structure one's experience in such a way as to provide the lessons one needs. Masonic Labour, in this sense, is an effort to live one's life according to principle so as to grow in terms of individual consciousness.

The first point to grasp about this sort of work is that when an individual starts he is usually working at the level of the Inner Guard or ego; thus, Masonic Labour starts with work on the ego. In the Ritual of Opening the Lodge the Inner Guard informs us that one of his duties is to be under the command of the Junior Warden. Considered in terms of the levels of consciousness represented by the Officers this means that the ego, symbolised by the Inner Guard, is to be under the command of some agency beyond the threshold of ordinary consciousness, the Junior Warden whom we have equated with the Self. The establishment of this command relationship is the first task for the Entered Apprentice. It is an important piece of work because the major activities of the individual's psyche, and his contact with Divinity, are accomplished through those higher levels of consciousness which are symbolised by the Junior Warden and the other Principal Officers. It is also a difficult task, because the Inner Guard/ego enjoys its role as boss (even though it is not particularly good at it) and it will devise all sorts of distractions to prevent the loss of that status.

We can consider some characteristics of the ego, to get an idea of the problems involved with establishing the Command Relationship. The ego is represented by a Door Keeper; and like most door keepers, it does not have a particularly broad perspective. Its task is to monitor the day-to-day routine psychological functions of thinking, feeling and acting and to present an acceptable face to the outside world. These two duties give a clue to the ego's limitations; it clings to routine and it is concerned with acceptability. As useful as these characteristics are in ordinary life, they are a source of difficulty when one attempts to place the ego under the control of the Self.

The ego's tendency to cling to routine is illustrated by the following example of a young woman who was working through this sort of problem in the context of her career. She was a very competent senior analyst in the field of information technology, who had resigned her position with a well established software house in order to pursue a career as a freelance consultant in the same field. She had recognised the need to 'stretch herself', and the desire to be her own boss was as much an influence in the decision as career progression. No sooner was she on her own, than she conceived the idea that the most important thing for her to do was to buy a personal computer and to set up a private data base of material relating to information technology. She reasoned that such a data base, which would require a year to establish, would be of great value in her work. Here we can see a person who was (and realised she was) an expert technician and who had decided to expand her capacity, broaden her scope, and assume additional responsibility for herself. This step into new territory promised to be an unsettling experience for her ego, and her ego responded by fixing on a project which was a repetition of the old pattern at which the ego was already expert. In fact, the most important thing for her to do was to go out and drum up some clients and learn to face up to the rough and tumble of commercial life. To do that, however, required that she come to grips with a part of her personality which she had not previously acknowledged. In spite of a friendly persona, she was quite shy and in the past when personal contact had become difficult she had always occupied herself with technical problems and passed the responsibility of coping with the world to her boss. It was a combination of good advice from friends and a shortage of money which forced her to stop tinkering with her computer, as her Inner Guard/ego would have been pleased to do, and get out to face the responsibilities which her Junior Warden/Self was offering. As well as illustrating the ego's preference for established routine this example illustrates its capacity to rationalise attractive distractions to keep itself in the comfortable situation of routine control.

The ego's concern with acceptability produces even more subtle obstacles to the establishment of the Command Relationship, and to understand them we will find it helpful to look briefly at how the ego develops normally. When the individual is born, the ego exists only in potential. Gradually, the infant begins to discover its body and to form a sense of itself as a being separate from the world around it and then to form concepts of various objects in that world. As the child grows, this sense which he has of himself, that is his ego, becomes better and better developed as he becomes more and more effective in answering the demands of his body while at the same time relating more skilfully to the world at large. As part of this process of relating to the world, the child learns to present an image of himself which is acceptable both to his concept of himself and to his associates; an image which enables him to relate to those around him, and prevents him from being attacked by them. This is the developing persona (in Jungian terms), and the behaviour by which the individual relates to the world and defends his psyche is the protective function which gives the Inner Guard his name. As we have seen, the individual may have many such personae, which are managed by the Inner Guard/ego and in this way the ego performs its proper role of permitting the individual to relate to the world while remaining secure and stable within himself. At the same time that the child's ego is developing the personalities which it shows the world, it is also learning from parents, teachers and associates those forms of behaviour which are acceptable and those which are not. Now all people have natural inclinations toward behaviour of various sorts and when the child is told that some of his behaviour is acceptable and some is not he tends to incorporate the acceptable behaviour into his developing personae and to put the desire for unacceptable behaviour out of his mind. For example, if a child has an aggressive nature and he is not given an acceptable way to release his aggressive energy but, rather, is told to behave himself, he may succeed in developing a peaceful, compliant persona while repressing his aggressive impulses. However, this inclination for aggression does not simply go away. We have seen that there is a principle in psychology (called the Rule of Three by the Craft) which says that energy will be distributed around the psyche in such a way as to keep things in balance. In the example we are considering the child's aggressive impulses reside in what will become his Shadow, in a part of the psyche which the ego has learned not to acknowledge and the Rule of Three operates (unconsciously) to invest as much energy in the repressed aggression as the child invests in his placid persona.

By the time the individual has completed adolescence the ego (Inner Guard) is usually well developed and operating more or less effectively. Most people enter adulthood with a set of personae which allows them to relate to their environment and with an equivalent amount of material stored in the Shadow. The majority of people live their entire lives in this situation; and never recognise the existence of the Shadow material, although it is often clearly visible to outside observers because the unconscious usually finds ways to express itself. Thus, to continue the example above, among genuinely peaceful people, one often finds professing pacifists who are involved in unlawful, often physically violent demonstrations against military installations and other symbols of authority as the content of their unconscious discharges some of its energy.

Now from the Craft's point of view, the development of the ego and personality outlined above is seen to be the development of that part of the psyche which relates to the physical world, controls the body, and provides an interface between the body and psyche proper. The psyche itself, the soul which incarnated, is seen to have existed all along (and may be quite mature). From this perspective the next step in normal development is the awakening of the awareness of the individual who has incarnated; that is, an awareness of the Self or the establishment of the Command Relationship of which we have been speaking.

The problem here is that the material which has been stored in the Shadow acts as a barrier between the ego and the Self. It forms a sort of rubble left over from the building of the Temple, which clutters up the Ground Floor and blocks the communication between the Inner Guard and the Junior Warden. In order to establish this Command Relationship one must clear out this rubble by becoming aware of the aspects of one's self that have been repressed, acknowledging them and, with the help of the Junior Warden/Self, integrating them into one's psyche. This is often a painful business because the ego has repressed the contents of the Shadow for the very reason that it was at one time considered unacceptable or even threatening. Here we should recall the words of the Master shortly after the admission of the candidate: 'avoiding fear on the one hand and rashness on the other, you will steadily persevere,' because in this connection they take on a new meaning. It takes real courage for a person who has built a notion of himself as loving, kind and considerate to recognise that he has a mean, selfish streak or one who has considered himself to be self-reliant to recognise that he avoids certain responsibilities. And, having recognised these things, it takes real perseverence to examine and work with these qualities until one has them under conscious control. Put another way, it requires that one be strictly honest with one's self and indeed the Command Relationship is called 'the Path of Honesty' in some traditions. Assistance in the task of establishing the Command Relationship comes from within, from the Junior Warden/Self and we can learn a good deal by examining that officer's situation.

Figure 5 shows the relationship of the four worlds, and the Junior Warden's position in this scheme is unique; he is located at the place where the three lower worlds meet. Thus, he is at the very pinnacle of the physical world and excellently placed to manage the subordinate functions of the incarnate psyche – to supervise the activity of the Ground Floor. At the same time he is at the centre of the psychological world – in intimate contact with his colleague, the Senior Warden or Soul – and he is at the lowest point of the Spiritual world – closely associated with the Master and his trans-personal perspective. It is this unique position which gives the Junior Warden/Self, the essence of the incarnate individual, its integrating capacity. In other traditions the Junior Warden is called the Watcher, or the Watchman in the Tower, to describe the alertness and enhanced perspective which is characteristic of that level of awareness. On occasion he is called the Guide, and perhaps it is in that capacity that we can experience him most easily and start to open the Command Relationship.

Everyone, at one time or another, experiences internal guidance. This guidance is not a simple feeling or hunch, it is clear knowledge, sometimes even a voice. Perhaps one is starting a romantic relationship and amidst the passion one hears quite clearly, 'I ought not to be doing this.' Or it may be that one is euphoric about a business venture which seems full of promise, but the voice says, 'This will end in disaster.' Sometimes it communicates encouragement, as when one is being urged to join a social gathering rather than start an important journey and the advice comes, 'You must go on that trip.' Counsel of this sort comes from the Junior Warden, the Self, which sees from its broader perspective. While one may have ignored such promptings in the past, a review of the advice received in this manner over the years will reveal that it was generally sound and had one been objective, it would have been seen to be obvious and common sense action at the time. After recognising that such guidance has been available, the next step in establishing the Command Relationship is to start to listen for the guidance. It actually comes frequently and the more one listens for it, the more one receives it. Often the advice is unpleasant and unwanted because, as we have seen, it will probably upset the Inner Guard's/ego's routine or invite its attention to something it does not wish to acknowledge. At such times one should remember one's promise as an Apprentice and persevere. On the other hand, nothing in interior work should be done without conscious awareness and it is important to evaluate the guidance which comes from the Junior Warden, particularly in the early stages. There are two criteria to use in this evaluation:

- does it make sense? and
- does it apply to me?

To answer both these questions requires that the Apprentice be absolutely honest with himself. Answering the first question honestly will teach him to examine situations from a broader perspective, and to learn to separate genuine guidance from the fantasy and wishful thinking which one sometimes receives. Answering the second question honestly will cause the Apprentice to examine his behaviour and attitudes and to come to grips with things about himself which his ego has avoided in the past.

As one considers the nature of this task, it becomes clear why our ancient brethren are said to have required seven years for the Apprentice's work. Habits and patterns of behaviour must change gradually; unpleasant truths about one's personality must be allowed to dawn slowly. Too sudden a realisation is a real shock, and too rapid a change can cause damage to the psyche. It is hard and, at times, unpleasant work to examine one's thoughts and behaviour objectively, but if one perseveres with honesty, the Command Relationship between Junior Warden and Inner Guard becomes well established and one finds that a source of excellent internal guidance is constantly available. Once the task is started, progress is facilitated by Providence which gives the Apprentice the opportunity to use his working tools.

The Working Tools

We have seen that one of the principal laws which operates within the Lodge/psyche is the Rule of Three which serves to maintain a balance between the active and passive psychological functions and within the psyche as a whole. We have also observed examples of how this law operates whether we are conscious of it or not. The Craft commits a good deal of its symbolic structure to elucidating the various aspects of the Rule of Three. It is represented in an overall perspective by the three pillars which extend through the Ground Floor, Middle Chamber and Holy of Holies of our human temple which suggests that the Rule operates throughout the psyche. In a more detailed fashion the Craft describes three agencies (active, passive and co-ordinating) which are said to be particularly characteristic of each Degree or psychological level. These three agencies are represented in each case by the Working Tools of the respective Degrees; that is the tools portray psychological functions which are characteristic of various psychological levels. Tools are appropriate symbols because the psychological functions, like the physical tools of a craftsman, must be mastered and put to purposeful use.

Before we proceed with our consideration of the tools of an Entered Apprentice it will be appropriate for us to examine a small bit of ritual which is associated with the presentation of the tools in each degree. The tools are always presented with the words 'but as we are not operative Masons, but speculative only'. This distinction between operative and speculative Masons is usually taken to refer to the difference between stone-cutters and philosophers; and so of course it does, at one level. We have seen, however, that the entire symbolic structure is an allegory of the psychological processes, and at that level the word 'operative' takes on a very different meaning. It refers not simply to the business of building in stone, but to the magical operations which occupied many scholars during the period when the Craft was evolving. A magical operation consists of so arranging things in the psychological world that the basic causality, operating from Divinity toward materiality (the East wind), produces a desired effect in the physical world. While such an idea may seem quaint from the perspective of twentieth-century materialism, it was a recognised capability in seventeenth-century England and the ritual is quite clear in its position on the subject: the speculative Craft deals with interior development; it is not involved with magical operations which attempt to influence the physical world. The position is restated in each degree at the time when the candidate receives the tools with which he can shape his psychological environment.

The tools of the Entered Apprentice are the Twenty-four-inch Gauge, the Common Gavel and the Chisel. As physical objects they are tools of action used for cutting stone, for doing things. That is appropriate, as they represent psychological functions to be used on the Ground Floor of the Temple, the part of the psyche in close relationship to the body.

The passive, containing psychological functions at the level of Action, are represented by the Chisel. We can see why this is when we examine the tool in use: it receives the blows of the stone-cutter, it is said to be of exquisite sharpness and to be related to education. From this symbolism we can infer that the Chisel represents the psychological functions of thought process: the analysis, classification, communication, storage, retrieval, sorting and presentation of data. These are all the mental faculties which are developed as one grows from the age of about seven to twelve years. If one observes children of this age, one sees that they are concerned with the acquisition of facts. They spend hours visiting museums acquiring detailed information about things or building gadgets which operate in some way. These activities teach the psyche to observe 'what it is, how it fits and how it works'. The games played by children of this age are highly structured and full of clever logic. Such games are to be played properly, not because of an interest in justice or any such broad issue, but because the rules themselves are important for their own sake.

It is also important to observe that the Chisel is a tool which works only on the surface of the stone. Thus, its effects are superficial in the same way that the analytical faculties of the psyche are superficial. Note that superficial does not mean trivial, indeed, the analytical faculties are very important, but by comparison with the issues of morality and identity which are treated in subsequent degrees they are superficial. (It is worth noting that the thought processes of the western industrial societies are heavily weighted in favour of this psychological function, which can be seen developed to its highest refinement in the academic discipline of information technology. The society's heavy emphasis on this psychological function may be a cause of many of the serious problems of the late twentieth century). By the time the child reaches twelve or thirteen years of age his capacity to analyse, classify and otherwise manipulate information (his Chisel, in other words) is more or less well developed and with the onset of adolescence he begins to develop his Gavel.

The Common Gavel which delivers the blows of the stone-cutter represents the psyche's active, expansive functions as experienced on the Ground Floor of the Temple. These active functions include one's passionate nature, psychological drives of all sorts, and all the cyclical, rhythmic activities of life. The emergence of this psychological faculty begins when changes in the child's body chemistry precipitate the onset of puberty. While the process is apparently started by this physical change, anyone who observes carefully the development of an adolescent realises very quickly that a great deal more is happening than the development of sexuality, although that certainly forms a large part of adolescent activity. Fascination with the games and devices of the analytical faculty is set aside as the capacity develops for strong feelings, for joy and rage, for physical prowess to be tested in athletic contests, for commitment to an ideal (even if, at this stage, the ideal is only a pop star), for rebellion against authority. The adolescent seldom stops to analyse or classify one experience before rushing on to the next. Rules are ignored in the urgency to satisfy the needs of the moment. This is a difficult time for everyone (particularly the adolescent himself) as all these driving impulses (Libido in Freudian terms) emerge into full consciousness for the first time. This is the Gavel of passion, the exact antithesis of the Chisel of analysis which developed in the previous phase. All this energy is of great importance to the individual in his everyday life as well as in his interior work. It is not to be suppressed or denied, but rather 'subdued', placed under control, so that it can be used as a tool in constructive tasks. By the time he has reached the age of about twenty-one the individual has experienced and, at least to some extent, assimilated the passionate side of his nature (his Gavel) in its various aspects. As we have seen earlier, it is at this time, after the two functional working tools of the First Degree are operational and available to the individual, that the work of the Craft can begin.

The Twenty-four-inch Gauge is an instrument of measurement and represents the mediating function which balances the other two. This co-ordinating faculty develops throughout the child's life as part of the development of the ego, and the early training in its use comes when the child learns that he cannot always have his own way, but must control his desires to fit in with the activities of his family. As the child enters adolescence and has to cope with the passionate side of his nature his Twenty-four-inch Gauge begins to work in earnest because successful adaptation to adolescent life requires substantial co-ordination between analysis and passion. For some, the co-ordination is pretty even-handed and they arrive at physical maturity with a reasonable balance of thought and feeling, although one function is usually favoured to some extent. However, for many, the co-ordination of these two functions during adolescence consists of suppressing one or the other; and such people start adult life at one extreme or the other, as flaming radicals out to change the world or as retiring bookworms who only wish to be left alone. The Lecture in the First Degree asks the question 'what come you here to do?' and the answer is 'to rule and subdue my passions and to improve myself in Masonry'. Here is the scope of the Labour in the First Degree. When the Apprentice first undertakes the work he finds, typically, that one of his Working Tools is over-developed at the expense of the other, and he is sometimes unaware that the co-ordinating function of the Twenty-four-inch Gauge is required at all. His task is to bring all these psychological functions first into experience and then under his conscious control. Note again that he is not to 'suppress' them, but to 'subdue and rule' them.

We have said that Masonry is an experience and in no area does that become obvious more quickly than in learning the use of these Working Tools. As soon as the Apprentice starts to establish the Command Relationship discussed in the previous chapter, Providence acts to provide circumstances in which the tools can be utilised. Some examples from real life will illustrate this process clearly. We will start with an experience which Jungian psychologists might call the differentiation of an archetype related to passion. It is the actual case of a middle-aged professor of information technology. He was a bachelor, having only briefly acknowledged an interest in girls. The demands of his PhD had required that he give all his attention to his computer studies, and as we should expect, the Rule of Three had ensured that there was an equivalent amount of energy invested in his passionate nature which was kept strictly out of his awareness. It revealed itself in his fervent dedication to both his studies and to his computer, and he was well established in his academic career. One day, as a result of an encounter at a friend's party, this professor found himself deeply involved in a love affair with a delightful and enthusiastically vigorous young woman, some ten years his junior. To his friends, the situation was a source of great amusement, and it was indeed the stuff of which television comedies are made. To him, however, it was a very serious situation. Suddenly brought face to face with the passionate side of his nature, which he had ignored for twenty-five years, his entire psychological processes were disrupted by the turbulent affair. His academic career was shaken because of the uncontrolled intrusion of the Gavel of passion into the analytical processes of his Chisel. Happily, he retained sufficient objectivity to recognise the need for some kind of balance in the situation. He persevered (as we would say) through the affair, eventually coming to grips with his passions and bringing them under his conscious control. After he had done that, he and his new wife could settle down to a rich and rewarding partnership.

Frequently, it is the Gavel which is the predominant function. Consider the case of a middle-aged English woman of great charm with well developed feelings and strong likes and dislikes which she imposed on her friends and acquaintances without hesitation, but with an aversion to analytical thinking. She was, in fact, formally involved in interior work to which she was fervently committed, and she offered to assist her teacher in the operation of his school. As it happened, her teacher was an extraordinarily wise and gentle individual in his eighties. He accepted his student's offer, and said that what the school really needed was an index to be prepared for the teacher's books which contained remarkably abstruse metaphysical text. Here we see an example of the situation in which a really kind and loving teacher assigns a distasteful task which is specifically designed to nurture the under-developed side of the student's psyche (in this case, the analytical faculty). This example does not have a happy ending. The student felt that the task was not well suited to her abilities (which was right enough, from her ego's point of view), and beneath her capabilities (which it was not). She declined to undertake the work, and went off in passionate pursuit of some other cause. The teacher, who was really a master of his craft, never offered an alternative assignment, although he kept the opportunity to write the index open as long as he remained alive.

We can derive several valuable lessons from these experiences, particularly from this failure. First, the tasks of Masonic Labour are presented by Providence, even though they may come through the agency of some individual. They are often difficult and distasteful. This is because the tasks are intended to develop a Working Tool or function which we have ignored or repressed and which does not perform well. Often, there are important, frequently painful, psychological reasons for the neglect. It is common that the under-developed function has no place in the personae which the ego uses to relate to the world, and the task which would develop the function is threatening to the ego. We, as the Apprentice who must perform the task, do not always appreciate the reasons which lie behind the assignments. We are frequently unaware of the function which needs developing, and our Inner Guard (ego) is often unwilling to admit that he has not done very well in co-ordinating our psychological activities. This is why perseverance is required and why the Command Relationship of Honesty between the Inner Guard and Junior Warden (ego and Self) is so important. It is also the reason for the Craft's insistence on 'a perfect submission to the Master and his Wardens whilst acting in the discharge of their respective offices'. The tasks of Masonic Labour are assigned by Providence and come to our awareness through the interior agencies symbolised by those officers. But there is even more to be learned from the rejected task. The teacher's forebearance and his willingness to let his student go about her own way is of great importance. A student may forego an opportunity and may find himself in serious difficulties because of it, but he always has the right to refuse the instruction. Even tasks arranged by Providence can be refused. Our professor could have abandoned his attractive friend, returned to his books and become a recluse. It had been a real temptation for him to do so, when his career began to suffer. In retrospect we can see that it would not have been to his benefit, but it was his right to do so. This refusal to perform a piece of Masonic Labour can be fatiguing, because, like the teacher who kept his offer open, Providence continues to present opportunities for growth in hopes that the student will wake up. One (or even several) refusals does not stop all progress. The Deity is very merciful in this respect and Providence, acting through the Principal Officers of our individual Lodge, keeps the door open and contrives to present opportunities for Masonic Labour which will develop a neglected working tool and bring it under conscious control. Repetitive behaviour is frequently an indicator that some process such as this is occurring. It is not uncommon for example, to know a person who has been in the same marriage three times. The names of the partners are different, but the situation is the same. Such a circumstance suggests that the person is ignoring an opportunity for personal development by refusing to grasp the lesson which 'life' (actually his own being) is presenting to him.

As the Apprentice Mason labours with his Chisel, Gavel and Gauge he finds that, slowly but inevitably, the expansive and containing side of his lower psyche come more and more into balance and his contact between the Inner Guard and the Junior Warden (ego and Self) becomes stronger. He finds that he reacts to situations less often and more frequently chooses his response. This is a sure sign of progress for the Apprentice and it raises the issue of free will and with it the subject of Testing by the Wardens.

4 TESTING BY THE WARDENS

It is generally assumed, at least in western democracies, that as long as he remains within the law, an adult human being is free to do as he chooses. We like to think we have free will. Indeed, as we have seen, freedom is one of the prerequisites for membership in the Craft. However, if we reflect a little on the content of the previous two sections, we will realise that while a man works at the level of the Inner Guard (ego) and as long as one of his working tools (either analysis or passion) heavily out-weighs the other, he has very little opportunity to choose the appropriate action, no matter what his legal rights may be. It is a fact that very few people have the opportunity to exercise free will because most are constrained by their own psychological processes. A complete discussion of the subject must include concepts introduced in the Second Degree, but the Apprentice's work starts the development of his will and an introduction will be useful.

While a person operates at the level of the Inner Guard he has very little personal freedom in a real sense. If such a person has a tendency to be passive, for example our academic bookworm (an Inner Guard with a well developed Chisel), he will tend to be will-less. That is, he will, pretty much, drift along with the crowd. If on the other hand, he tends to be active, to behave in an aggressive manner which demands that he achieve his objectives (an Inner Guard with a well developed Gavel) he will tend to be will-full. That is, he will try to impose his way on everyone about him. Each of these people will say, 'That's the sort of bloke I am', but in truth, they are each driven by their well developed side and simply cannot behave otherwise. More seriously, people who are in such a situation are open to manipulation by others who choose to do that sort of thing. Examples are easy to cite. It might be a church which exhorts people to undertake a crusade, a government which mobilises an army against a neighbour, or a trade union which calls its members out on a strike contrary to their interests. In each case people respond without thinking (because part of their psychological processes are not available to their consciousness) while believing that they act from free will.

When the Apprentice turns his attention inward, toward the Junior Warden (his Self) and when he begins to recognise and cultivate both the active and passive sides of his nature, then his attitude changes to one of willingness. This willingness is willing to be open to interior guidance from the Principal Officers of one's Lodge. As he becomes increasingly more honest with himself, as the Command Relationship between Junior Warden and Inner Guard becomes stronger and as the Working Tools of analysis and passion come into balance, he begins to have a real choice about how he behaves. That ability to choose is the beginning of what the Apprentice may properly call 'my will'. This is as far as we can take this analysis at the moment, but we can note that with the emergence of his own will comes not only the ability to choose, but also the responsibility to choose well and the opportunity to choose badly. It is because of this opportunity to exercise conscious choice which may be intentionally wrong that the Wardens test the Apprentice.

Like the labour which develops the tools, the tests come in the form of real-life experiences which are arranged by Providence to probe at the Apprentice's weakest points. A single example will suffice. Our friend, the professor of information technology, by now happily married, had reached a critical point in his career and recognised that some advancement was needed if he was not to stagnate professionally. At this critical juncture, and while his wife was away visiting her family, one of his attractive students offered herself for a romantic liaison. The control of the passionate side of his nature was one of his newest and least well developed skills and this offer proved to be a powerful attraction to his recently developed Gavel. That is the nature of temptation, and it took the greatest discipline he could exercise for our professor to pass by the offer. In the following week, the dean of the school in which the professor taught made a casual remark at a meeting. Our friend sensed an opportunity. His response led to a conversation and eventually to a promotion at a different university. Only in retrospect did our friend recognise the internal test, and realise that had he been caught up in the emotional turmoil and guilt of an illicit affair, he would have missed the implication in his dean's remark and never recognised the opportunity which led to the next step in his development. This event gives us a clue into a process which we will examine later. This is temptation and its purpose is to ensure that people do not grow into situations which they cannot handle.

If the labour is long and arduous, the Warden's testing is extremely subtle. It is very important, however, because as the Apprentice acquires the ability to choose, as he 'awakens', he acquires a proportional ability to do real harm if he chooses for selfish reasons. These trials which test the integrity of the Apprentice are as frequent as they are subtle. They are the 'repeated trials and approbations' by which the ritual says one knows oneself to be a Mason, and once they start, they continue throughout one's life. When one considers Masonic Labour as it has been defined in these last sections, one can understand better the admonitions for perseverance and the reason for allocating seven years for the work. None the less, if the Apprentice does persevere, the relationship between his Inner Guard and Junior Warden (ego and Self) becomes very close, his active and passive functions at Ground Floor level become finely tuned and responsive, and he becomes aware that he is increasingly choosing to control his activities. When the Apprentice was symbolically initiated into the Craft, the sun was said to have been at the Meridian. The reference is to the Junior Warden who represents the sun in that position, and when his real moment of initiation occurs the Apprentice experiences a new perspective which is of that brilliant nature. Now, with his Command Relationship well established, his consciousness exhibits that clarity as a general rule. To the world at large, such a person will be known as a good and thoughtful man, and it is time for him to begin the serious work of the Craft.

Now is the time at which he must exercise the third right of an Entered Apprentice. He must petition his Lodge for the Second Degree. His Lodge, as we understand it, is the interior of his psyche, and when he is ready, an event occurs which in the Craft is symbolised by the Ceremony of Passing.

CHAPTER 4
The Middle Chamber

1 THE NATURE OF WORK IN THE SECOND DEGREE

The Fellowcraft Degree is a much misunderstood and neglected part of
the Masonic Order. The ceremony is brief and simple and unless it is
administered by Masons who have some insight into the interior meaning
of the Work it must inevitably appear to be relatively unimportant. In
fact, exactly the opposite is the case; and much of the major work of the
Craft (understood from the perspective we have adopted here) is to be
accomplished in this Degree. As an Apprentice we have seen that one
works on the Ground Floor, in close relation with the body to bring the
lower part of one's psyche into balance and under control. As a Master
Mason one will work in King Solomon's Porch adjacent to the Holy of
Holies, in close relation with the Spirit, to bring the influence of that
realm into conscious experience. But here, in the Middle Chamber, is an
area which exists entirely within the psyche, between the Physical and
Spiritual worlds as Figure 5 indicates. This is the Soul, the essence of the
individual, and the Work to be accomplished in the Soul – in the
Middle Chamber – is essential if one is to progress further. There are at
least two reasons why the Degree is presented in a low key. First,
because, important as it is, work on the psyche should not be considered
as important in itself. Rather it should only be undertaken as intentional
preparation for the Third Degree. We have noted that it is one of the
fundamental notions of the Craft that interior development of the
individual should not be undertaken for personal benefit or, indeed, for
any purpose other than service to the Deity. That is one of the reasons
for the Craft's continued emphasis on charity. 'A genuine desire for
knowledge and a sincere wish to render yourself more extensively
serviceable to your fellow creatures', were the motives which enabled
the candidate to enter the Craft, and the same purity of motive is
required of the Fellowcraft. The exploration of the psyche for purpose
of personal gain is considered by the Craft to be improper. Second, the
work is interior work. It occurs deep within the psyche in the 'hidden

pathways of Nature and Science'. In one of the American Jurisdictions the Ritual of Opening asks of a Fellowcraft Lodge:

'When of but five, of whom does it consist?'
'The Worshipful Master, Senior and Junior Wardens, and the Senior and Junior Deacons.'

Notice that the officers whose task it is to relate the individual to the physical world are not active in a Fellowcraft Lodge (or, more precisely, they are active, but do not obtrude into consciousness at this level). It is to this interior work, to the discovery of 'hidden pathways of Nature and Science', that the candidate is introduced at the Ceremony of Passing.

2 THE CEREMONY OF PASSING

The Ceremony of Passing from the Entered Apprentice to the Fellowcraft Degree starts with an examination of proficiency in the former Degree. In the real-life event, which is symbolised by the Ceremony of Passing, this examination is accomplished as part of the almost constant testing that one experiences when one starts one's interior development. This testing is referred to as 'repeated trials and approbations' in the Lectures, and is represented by the frequent 'proving' of brethren and candidates which is to be found in the rituals. The examination prior to Passing differs from the other tests only in that it leads directly to an advance in the scope of one's work and awareness. In fact, the experience of our friend the professor, which we examined at the end of the previous section, was such a test, since it preceded a change in career which actually facilitated his interior growth.

Passing, as a verb used to describe the movement from First to Second Degree, is a word chosen with great care. Just as 'initiation' implies a completely new start and 'raising' implies an elevation to a new and higher level, so 'passing' implies the gaining of some milestone, but while pursuing the same path one has been following. Masonically the event of Passing indicates real progress but it is a slow, gentle, natural process of unfoldment which bears its fruit in its own time. This concept is communicated to the candidate by the ear of corn with which he is presented upon completion of his test of proficiency. The grain symbolises the natural, unforced, psychological growth which has occurred as a result of the patient work in the First Degree. Like the maturation of the grain, this growth derives from a hidden source and it bears fruit in its own season – it cannot be hurried. The ear of corn also draws attention to the parallel between the natural development of the grain after the plant is mature and the natural unfoldment of the psyche after the body is mature.

When the candidate enters the lighted Fellowcraft's Lodge his vision (symbolic of his psychological perception) is unimpaired. This indicates that the faculties he already possesses will suffice him for the work of this degree. This is a marked contrast to his previous situation in which he was blind to (unaware of) the subject upon which he was to enter, and from this we can infer that in the Second Degree one will continue to work in the psyche as one has done in the First. That is indeed the case, as in this degree one is 'permitted to extend' one's researches. The area for research is indicated, at the time of the candidate's reception, by the use of the Square.

The Square is used in the Craft's ritual in at least four different contexts; in all of them it refers in some way to the psyche. It is one of the Three Great Lights, and in that composite symbol of the three upper worlds it represents the psyche, or World of Formation. As one of the Movable Jewels it facilitates testing the work of the Craftsman. As a Working Tool in the Second Degree it defines the relationship between the other two tools. In the reception of the candidate, the Square it refers to is one quarter of something, that thing being symbolised by a circle. Now the circle is an almost universal symbol for the whole of existence, the relative universe which contains four worlds according to our cosmology. The 'fourth part of a circle' defines one of the four worlds. The purpose of this reception is to inform the candidate that the work of this Degree takes place entirely within the psyche, the World of Forms. The manner of his reception also indicates that the candidate will be dealing with matters which relate to the heart, the level of emotion (as distinguished from the feelings, which were considered in the First Degree).

As the candidate passes round the Lodge and is examined by the Wardens as part of their ceaseless task of testing, his use of the password gives him a clue about the nature of the progress he has made (although he will be unable to interpret this clue properly until he has heard the Lecture of the Second Degree). That Lecture describes the circumstances under which the password was first used and a little research into the Ammonitish War is instructive. The Ephraimites had been asked to assist in that conflict and had declined, leaving Gilead to fight alone. Thus, in the event referred to in the ritual, the Ephraimites were in Gilead, where they had no business to be, to take by force something to which they were not entitled and for which they had not fought (laboured). The password by which they were discovered alludes to 'an ear of corn'. When we look at the passage from the perspective of interior development we can recognise Ephraimites as those who do not possess the psychological maturity which is the result of labour in the First Degree. The candidate, who by virtue of his labours is in possession of the maturity symbolised by an ear of corn, can understand that he has gained admission to a place (level of consciousness) which would previously have been dangerous for him (and is still dangerous for those whose 'ear of corn' is not yet mature). In the Craft the password is used to 'prevent any unqualified person from ascending the winding staircase which led to the Middle Chamber of the Temple'. We can see that the concern is for the protection of the unqualified as well as of the Fellowcraft.

The obligation is so brief as to be almost disappointing to the casual observer. After the admonitions for secrecy of which we have already spoken, the only new obligations are to be a 'true and faithful Craftsman' and to 'answer signs and obey summonses'. Before one passes off these new responsibilities as trivial one should stop and consider from where it is that signs and summonses originate. They originate, of course, from other Fellowcrafts and from Lodges of Fellowcraft Freemasons, but we have seen that a Lodge is the model of an individual's interior being. A summons from such a 'Lodge' is very different from the Secretary's note advising one of a meeting. As we shall see, a Fellowcraft Freemason (in the real sense) is a very remarkable person and many people – Masons and non-Masons alike – will 'recognise the sign' and know the real Fellowcraft to be a person to whom they can turn for help about their problems in the world. It is in this context that one must 'answer summonses' and be 'true and faithful'. As soon as one has gained even a little insight, the obligation for charity incurred in the north-east corner during one's Initiation begins to operate, and that obligation must be discharged faithfully.

The expanded awareness of the Second Degree carries the privileges of research into the deeper psyche and, like all privileges, these carry responsibilities. Therefore, the Second Degree's obligation, like its predecessor, is associated with a traditional penalty, which describes the attendant risk; and, like its predecessor, this penalty is allegorical. It refers to a process to which one's psyche becomes susceptible if one fails to conduct one's self properly at this level of activity – if one ignores or betrays the trust of one seeking help or instruction. As the physical symbols of the penalty relate to the heart, so the allegory refers to the 'things of the heart', the emotional and moral level of the psyche. Improper conduct by a Fellowcraft (in the sense that we are considering here) will certainly lead to a deterioration of the psyche at the emotional level, and, if persisted in, to severe psychological disorders. In the old days such disorders were called possession by demons. Today they may be called severe psychotic states. C. G. Jung was among the first to point out that the symptoms are similar (often the same), although the mechanism of such disturbances is still little understood, even by contemporary psychologists.

Once again, the Candidate's attention is drawn to the Three Great Lights, which we have seen to be representative of the three upper worlds. The altered configuration of these objects indicates that he can now (or will, as he works in this Degree) begin to perceive, in part, the spirit which underlies the form with which he works. Among the old building trades, from which the Craft borrows its symbols, a Fellow of the Craft was a man who could read and understand the plan and raise a building from it. We can infer a similar level of competence for a Mason of the Second Degree. For us the configuration of the Great Lights indicates that the Fellowcraft can read and understand the Divine Plan sufficiently well to co-operate intelligently in its implementation. As we have said, he is likely to be a remarkable person.

The signs of the Fellowcraft which the candidate receives at this stage are not simply identifiers, as in the First Degree, but also devices for instruction (by way of reminders) to the Fellowcraft himself. They do, however, identify the individual. As we have noted in connection with the First Degree, Masonic signs, as plain physical gestures, are simply emblematic of qualities which mark the individual who possesses them. In the case of the Fellowcraft, there are several such qualities, and one wonders how 'secret' these real signs can really be. As we have seen, the qualities symbolised by Masonic signs do not necessarily identify one as a Mason, rather as a person of a certain level of interior development. Many people recognise one who has reached the level of awareness symbolised by the Fellowcraft Degree by sensing that here is a person to be trusted, since trustworthiness is one of the 'signs'. It is from this recognition that many 'summonses' originate. A second of these intangible qualities is steadfastness, so that those who seek the assistance of a Fellowcraft (be he a Mason or not) feel confident that he will not abandon them at a critical time. For the individual Fellowcraft these signs carry instruction too. The trustworthy quality does not simply refer to secrets of the Order. A person who researches into himself and who exhibits the quality of trustworthiness acquires substantial personal capability, and that makes him an object of interest to a variety of agencies to which the Craft refers as the 'insidious'. We will investigate these agencies in due course, but for the Fellowcraft the signs are a reminder to be true to himself, too. In a similar way his steadfast, persevering quality reminds him that the Fellowcraft Degree is an interim state, and that he himself is in a process of transition – a transition which is always finely balanced and which he is obligated to himself to complete if he would avoid serious personal difficulties.

The badge of a Fellowcraft, like that of an Entered Apprentice, represents the candidate's psychological vehicle, the 'body' with which he inhabits the psychological world. He receives it from the Senior Warden, as he must, because that Officer represents the Soul which enclothes the Spirit while it remains in the World of Forms. The Fellowcraft's badge differs from the Entered Apprentice's in two important respects. First, the manner in which it is worn indicates an increased degree of integration within the candidate's psyche. This is a reflection of the individual's mundane activities (represented by the quadrilateral figure) being open to and receiving the influence of the conscious application of the Rule of Three (represented by the triangular figure). Second, the decorations on the badge reflect the development and maturation of the psychological vehicle. That is a process which will continue as the Fellowcraft pursues his investigation of the 'hidden mysteries of Nature and Science'.

Before he leaves the Lodge, the new Fellowcraft is given his Working Tools. We will defer their analysis until the section on Labour in the Second Degree. At the moment, it is worth noting that they are all instruments which measure by making comparison against absolute criteria – such a comparison is the nature of morality. Note also that, although the Apprentice is represented as a Rough Ashlar or building stone, the Perfect Ashlar does not represent the Fellowcraft. That state of perfection is representative of a stage of consciousness significantly more refined than that of the competent craftsman. However, the Perfect Ashlar is available in the Fellowcraft's Lodge 'for the experienced Craftsman to try and adjust his tools on'. The work of the Second Degree relates to morality, and the absolute standard for that morality is to be found within each individual, in his Middle Chamber – his Soul.

Of the many other symbols available to the Fellowcraft, one must claim our attention here. It is the letter 'G'. This character is present in the Lodge at all times but is emphasised in the Fellowcraft Lodge. In some Lodges the letter is dark until the Lodge is opened in the Second Degree, at which time it is illuminated. In others, it is not mentioned except in the ritual of the Second Degree. In both cases, the intention is the same – to point out a fact of which the individual cannot be conscious until he has reached the level of awareness symbolised by the Fellowcraft. The initial relates to the Name of God, in the same way that the Name appears on the Second Degree Tracing Board, and its presence in the Middle Chamber teaches that Divinity resides within each human being. Note that like the symbol in the Lodge, Divinity is always present in everyone, waiting to be recognised. Its presence is not something which membership in the Craft brings about. Participation in Masonic Labour (or some comparable discipline) simply enables one to become aware of it. Note also that the symbol is not the presence of Divinity itself. The level of consciousness represented by the Second Degree is not ready for that experience. It is the Initial, the Name of Divinity, a representation of the Divine Reality. The individual who actually enters that part of his psyche represented by the Middle Chamber sees this symbol and knows that deep within the centre of the Temple of his being, Divinity itself is to be found. In the words of one of the Teachers in the Volume of Sacred Law, 'The Kingdom of Heaven is within you.'

There is a long road ahead of the new Fellowcraft, if he is ever to reach that central place. To walk that road, he must continue his Masonic Labour and, like the Apprentice before him, the Craftsman needs instruction. That is to be found in the Lecture and Tracing Board, and there we shall look before considering Labour in the Second Degree.

3 SECOND DEGREE CONCEPTS

Cosmology

We have noted the simplicity of the Second Degree ritual which has often caused it to be neglected or at least regarded as of secondary importance in the Craft's system. This misleading simplicity is reflected in the Charge to the Fellowcraft, which is almost disappointing in its brevity. Beyond recommending continued attention to the elaborate advice given him as an Apprentice, the Charge in the Second Degree simply 'observes' that the candidate is 'now permitted to extend his researches into the more hidden mysteries of Nature and Science.' The ceremony does not even comment on what those mysteries might be. If the ritual in the Second Degree is simple, we must assume that it was structured in that fashion for some purpose; because the principal material of the Degree (which is both rich, and broad in scope) is contained not in the ritual, but in the Lecture. This is entirely appropriate because Work in the Middle Chamber, one's Soul, is essentially interior work and must, necessarily, tend to emphasise the approach of contemplation over that of ritual. With this in mind, we will consider the Lecture for some clue to the nature of the hidden mysteries into which the new Fellowcraft may now research. Of the five sections of the Second Lecture, one recapitulates the ceremony and three discuss the symbolism of the Tracing Board. The remaining (second) section introduces three apparently unconnected subjects: Geometry, Travel and Creation. We will look at the Tracing Board in the next chapter, but here we will confine our attention to the second section of the Lecture. As we do so it will be useful to keep two things in mind. First, although the Lectures are said to be explanatory, that is hardly the case. It is more accurate to say that they introduce material for study, and they often do that by the merest hint. Second, the material in the Lectures was originally addressed to Englishmen living in the seventeenth and eighteenth centuries, and if it is to be interpreted properly, it must be seen in the context of that period. This puts a double burden on the twentieth-century Mason. He must understand what the Craft's symbols meant to their intended recipients before he can apply them to himself.

The three topics which require our attention in the second section of the Lecture are Geometry, Creation and Travel. At first glance they appear to be quite separate subjects, which gives the Lecture a discontinuous quality. As we examine them here, however, it will become clear that they are but three important aspects of a single subject, western metaphysical cosmology, to which the new Fellowcraft is to be introduced. We touched on this subject when we introduced the doctrine of the four worlds and we will not repeat all that material here; but it will be useful to see how the Craft introduces other related concepts which we have been using.

The candidate is said to have been passed to the Second Degree 'for the sake of Geometry' which is defined as 'a science whereby we find out the contents of bodies unmeasured by comparing them with those already measured'. The subjects are said to include 'a regular progression of science from a point to a line, from a line to a superficies, and from a superficies to a solid.' This is certainly an incomplete, perhaps even inaccurate, definition of Geometry. Even considering the language of the seventeenth century, mathematical concepts were defined with greater precision than the lecture exhibits and this incompleteness should lead us to look further for a different meaning which is accurately stated. The first quotation, while incomplete in the mathematical sense, is a very nice statement of the old principle of interior work, 'If you want to understand the invisible, observe the visible.' This principle, which we have been using throughout the book, is based on the Law of Unity, and it suggests that there is a single set of laws operating throughout the four worlds which comprise the relative universe. When we see them operate to produce observable results in the physical (visible) world we can be sure that the same laws are operating in an analogous way in the psychological and spiritual worlds because the laws themselves take their origin in the Divine World. As we have observed before, the most succinct statement of this principle is 'As above, so below'. We have seen that the second quotation is a direct reference to the doctrine of the Four Worlds which we developed in Chapter 1, Section 3. It was a reasonably common idiom in neo-platonic literature and we may assume that the seventeenth-century Mason would have come across it in his readings and would recognise the context. Should the new Fellowcraft not be familiar with neo-platonic literature, the Lecture pointed him in that direction by informing him that 'Geometry was founded as a science' in Alexandria by Euclid. Actually, Geometry was practised in Greece by Pythagoras who was about two hundred years Euclid's senior. The questionable accuracy might be rationalised by arguing the meaning of 'founded as a science', but it is more fruitful to ask why the framers of the Lecture chose to emphasise Euclid and Alexandria. The passage is almost certainly a pointer, because the enquiring Craftsman who turned his attention to Alexandria would surely have found neo-platonism, since that city was the site of one of the most important neo-platonic schools. Similarly, if he turned to Euclid in the seventeenth and early eighteenth centuries he would find John Dee's famous introduction to the English translation; and that, as we have seen, guides him directly into the

Hermetic/Kabbalistic tradition, part of the main-stream of Renaissance thought.

Once we have seen the subject of Geometry and the geometric progression as a device for introducing the doctrine of the Four Worlds its relationship to the Creation story becomes clear. In fact, each is drawn from substantially the same source. The Lecture's illustration of the seven periods of Creation is a summary of the first two chapters of Genesis – the first of the five books of Moses. The Geometric progression as a representation of the Four Worlds is taken from an eleventh-century Kabbalistic work which covers the same material and includes part of the old Jewish oral tradition as well. The Lecture uses these two references to describe the structure of the relative universe; the processes by which it was created, formed and made, and some of the approaches by which it can be understood. A critical reading of the first two chapters of Genesis is rewarding for the Fellowcraft. It is instructive, not only because it gives an indication of the processes by which the Four Worlds unfold, but it also gives a brief glimpse into the structure of the World of Creation, the Spiritual World. The seven periods of creation describe seven levels within the Spiritual World. They are analogous to the seven levels in the psyche which the Craft defines by the seven Officers of the Lodge.

Taken together these two references, Geometry and Creation, encapsulate much of the essence of western metaphysical cosmology. Two other references make the Craft's cosmology complete. In any God-centred system causality is a fundamental element and it is incorporated into the Craft by the symbol of the Wind. The Wind is introduced in the Lecture of the First Degree as a Divine Instrument, the east wind which parted the Red Sea and saved the Children of Israel from the Egyptian army. This wind, which is also said to 'refresh men at labour', is considered to be favourable when blowing due east and west. There are several points in this image which enable us to integrate it into our Masonic model. We have seen that east-west is the 'dimension of consciousness', and we have observed that the World of the Spirit is related to the element Air, while the psyche is the Watery World. Now, the Book of Exodus and the journey from Egypt to Caanan from which the incident at the Red Sea is taken is itself an allegory of the psychological process which the Craft represents as temple-building. (For a contemporary Kabbalistic interpretation of this subject see Z'ev ben Shimon Halevi, *Kabbalah and Exodus*, Rider, 1980). In this context one sees parting of the waters as the result of the Divine Will, acting through the agency of the Spirit (air) to produce an effect in the psyche (water). The Craft puts the event in a broader context as one example of the favourable east wind, and in this way defines its direction of causality from east to west, from Divinity toward the physical world.

The final concept, which completes the Craft's allegory of the relative universe, is the introduction of man into the model. Man is pictured as a traveller; indeed, in some parts of the world the term 'travelling man' is a guarded synonym for a Mason. The concept of travelling is found in all three degrees and the road is always the same – the east-west direction, which tells us that the Mason's journey is taken through the stages of consciousness. The Apprentice travels from the materiality of the west and aspires to a consciousness of Divinity in the east. This is a relatively straightforward idea and we have seen how the work of an Apprentice starts him on that journey. The Fellowcraft has made some progress in the easterly direction and has access to the Middle Chamber, his Soul. In this intermediate state he is said to travel east to receive instruction, by which we can infer that when one withdraws to the level of consciousness represented by the Soul, one gains valuable insights. He also travels west to teach, which gives us some idea of the responsibility that a little progress in the work imposes. The Master Mason comes from the East where he is conscious of the presence of Divinity. While teaching is part of his task, he is more directly concerned with an issue of much greater scope as we shall see in due course. Through these three different references to travelling, man is presented as a being who is able to operate in all Four Worlds, to experience the entire spectrum of consciousness represented by the east-west dimension.

In the brief paragraphs above we have seen how the Craft defines the 'hidden mysteries of Nature and Science', and a little reading into the seventeenth-century literature on the subject will give a clear picture of the scope (if not the content) of the field into which the Fellowcraft was expected to research. Like the Craft itself, we will say little on the nature of this research beyond noting that one who works at the (actual) Fellowcraft level can expect to develop capacities which are presently classified as paranormal phenomena. These capacities are highly individual and are related to a particular person and to the task which he must accomplish in this life. Generally speaking, they do not emerge until an individual has achieved a substantial amount of psychological integration. To understand how that integration comes about we must consider the concepts introduced by the Second Degree Tracing Board.

4 THE SECOND DEGREE TRACING BOARD

The Staircase

The Tracing Board of the Second Degree is a detailed drawing of a part of the general domain depicted on the First Degree Tracing Board. Looking carefully at the latter we have seen that it shows two things, which are designed to the same plan. The first, consisting of the Floor, Columns, Heavens and Glory, is a picture of the Psychological World, and this picture is shown in some detail. The second (which is more general and more diagrammatic) consists of the Point-within-a-circle-bounded-by-two-parallel-lines, the Ladder and the Glory. It is a representation of the individual, incarnate human being, and shows his relationship to the relative universe. In this latter diagram the two parallel lines and the Ladder correspond to the Three Columns in the larger drawing, while the circle represents the potential radius of the incarnate individual's consciousness. It is this second diagram, this view of the individual psyche, which is expanded in the Second Degree Tracing Board.

The central object on the Board is the Winding Staircase, which is said to contain three, five and seven (or more) steps. It is depicted between two pillars which are described as having opposite characteristics. We will examine these pillars, which relate to the active and passive psychological functions, in the next section. Here we will give our attention to the Pillar of Consciousness, represented on the Board by the Winding Stairs. As we will see, the symbolic structure of the staircase is relatively complex. Generally speaking the Second Lecture associates various ideas with each group of steps: the central characters in the Hiramic Legend with the three, the Noble Orders of Architecture with the five, and the Liberal Arts and Sciences with the seven. These associations seem straightforward, but their implications require careful interpretation. We will start with a comment on the three sets of ideas which the Lecture associates with the groups of steps.

The Seven Liberal Arts and Sciences were recommended, almost in passing, to the Entered Apprentice. Now, when the new Fellowcraft receives his badge, he is told that 'you are expected to make the liberal arts and sciences your future study.' These subjects comprised the curricula at medieval universities and were divided into two parts. The Trivium contained the Arts – Grammar, Logic and Rhetoric – and was studied by undergraduates. The Quadrivium contained the Sciences –

Arithmetic, Geometry, Music and Astronomy – and these comprised the graduate curriculum. As these seven subjects are still studied today, the modern Mason has a tendency to interpret them in contemporary terms, something which the originators of the Lecture certainly did not have in mind. In fact the material recommended to the seventeenth- and eighteenth-century Mason, for whom the Lectures was intended, is intimately connected with the Hermetic/Kabbalistic tradition upon which we touched when we looked at the historical background of the Craft. This is as we might expect, since that was a mainstream of Renaissance thought. Even a brief analysis of the Liberal Arts and Sciences is far beyond the scope of this book, but two small examples will indicate the unexpected content of the curriculum. The subject of Rhetoric contained formal memory training which was originally intended to enable Roman politicians, who did not have writing materials for note-taking, to remember and respond to complex arguments during lengthy debates. By the time of the Renaissance this aspect of Rhetoric had developed into a substantial body of literature which incorporated the principles of the Hermetic/Kabbalistic tradition, a literature which was virtually contemporary with the formulators of the Craft (F. A. Yates, *The Art of Memory*, Ark edition, 1984). Astronomy, too, has changed its meaning since the seventeenth century, and we must realise that to the founders of our Order the word implied what we would call Astrology today. Before we dismiss material of this sort as superstition, we should remember that C. G. Jung has shown that much of it is a symbolic representation of psychological processes which occur in the unconscious, and our contemporary knowledge does not invalidate it when it is interpreted from this point of view.

In a similar way, the Noble Orders of Architecture represent more than we might initially expect and more than we can analyse here. We must be content to note that as soon as one starts to study them one meets Vitruvius, the Roman architect who codified the orders by classifying existing structures and formalising their proportions. Proportion was of great importance to Vitruvius, who advanced the idea that well designed buildings, and particularly temple buildings, should incorporate proportions derived from the human form. This concept is based on the principle, with which we should be familiar by now, that man is a microcosm, the reflection of the universal macrocosm, and the image of Divinity. Vitruvius' writings had a profound effect on Renaissance architecture and on the thinking of such men as Giorgi, Agrippa and Dee, who quotes liberally from Vitruvius in his famous preface to Euclid. Thus Vitruvius, the practical builder, is also seen to be a philosopher; and the Renaissance scholars saw him, and the architecture he promulgated, to be a description of the building of the 'inner temple' of one's own psyche.

The Arts and Sciences and the Noble Orders of Architecture referred the early Fellowcraft to material which was available as contemporary (or at least relatively recent) literature. By contrast, the Lecture's reference to the three principal characters in the Hiramic Legend directed the candidate's attention to the Craft's own symbolic structure. We will consider that Legend in due course; at the moment we may simply note the roles played by each central character:

- Solomon, King of Israel, had the idea, was the inspiration for the project, and provided overall direction in building the temple.
- Hiram, King of Tyre, facilitated the project by providing the means – the physical capacity.
- Hiram Abiff supervised the work and saw to it that the task was accomplished.

This briefest glimpse into the vast body of material referenced in the fourth section of the Second Lecture must suffice for our purpose here. Superficial as it is, it shows how the Lecture refers the Fellowcraft to the Hermetic/Kabbalistic line of Renaissance thought; and the Craftsman who examines that literature today will certainly find the effort rewarding. It also gives us the framework within which to apply these subjects to the Winding Stairs, and it is to that symbol that we now give our attention.

In addition to the associations mentioned above, the Lecture relates the Stairs to the seven Officers of the Lodge. Specifically, it relates the three steps to the Three Principal Officers who comprise a Master Mason's Lodge; the five steps to those three plus two Fellowcrafts (in some rituals, the Deacons) who form a Fellowcraft's Lodge; and the seven steps to those five plus the two Entered Apprentices (in some rituals, the Guards) who make up an Entered Apprentice's Lodge and make the whole structure perfect, that is, complete. The really significant thing about these groupings applied to the stairs is that they are not discrete, rather, the smaller are contained within the larger. That is, the group of three is contained within the five, and the group of five is contained within the seven. In other words, there are seven people in these groups – not fifteen. These overlapping groups provide a clue to the meaning of a *winding* stair. A staircase which winds covers the same ground with every turn; and the Second Lecture covers the same ground as it comments, from three different perspectives, on the levels of consciousness represented by the Seven Officers. So we see that:

- The three principal characters in the Hiramic Legend are associated with the Three Principal Officers.
- The Five Noble Orders of Architecture are associated with the Principal Officers and the Deacons.
- One of the Seven Liberal Arts and Sciences is related to each of the Seven officers.

This notion is represented schematically in Figure 7. We have already considered the Officers as a hierarchy of consciousness, while introducing the Craft's model of the psyche. The concept derives from this interpretation of the Winding Stairs as an alternative representation of the central pillar of Wisdom on the Second Degree Board. We will look at it again, now, and incorporate this additional material.

We have called the Tyler the consciousness of the Body/Physical World, and we have touched on how his role as a guard reflects his task in limiting the volume of external stimuli which are allowed to impinge on the psyche. The Art associated with this level of consciousness is Grammar. Now Grammar is a mechanical discipline. It does not deal with thinking, rather, its function is to permit the individual who has already formulated his thoughts to communicate them to others with ease and precision. Thus, Grammar has to do with establishing and maintaining the relationship between the individual and his social environment. Note that the aspect of body consciousness represented by Grammar is outwardly directed and has to do with establishing a relationship with the environment. In this sense it is complementary to the Guard's defensive role which limits that relationship. Note also that Grammar is a highly structured subject, and by associating it with the Outer Guard the model suggests that one's relationship with the external world should be a disciplined and controlled process of giving and receiving.

We have seen the Inner Guard to represent ego consciousness which, according to Freud's view, is charged with the business of satisfying one's desires (pleasure principle) within the limitations imposed by one's environment (reality principle). The Art associated with the Inner Guard is Logic, which has to do with the ordered use of one's analytical faculty. It is an essential ingredient of successful activity in the everyday

Winding Stairs

        Solomon, King of Israel (Worshipful Master)
       Hiram, King of Tyre (Senior Warden)
     Hiram Abiff (Junior Warden)
       Ionic Order (Worshipful Master)
      Doric Order (Senior Warden)
     Corinthian Order (Junior Warden)
    Composite Order (Senior Deacon)
   Tuscan Order (Junior Deacon)
       Astronomy (Worshipful Master)
      Music (Senior Warden)
     Geometry (Junior Warden)
    Arithmetic (Senior Deacon)
   Rhetoric (Junior Deacon)
  Logic (Inner Guard)
 Grammar (Tyler)

Compacted into Seven Steps

            Worshipful Master   (Spirit)
             Solomon, King of Israel
             Ionic Order
             Astronomy
         Senior Warden   (Soul)
          Hiram, King of Tyre
          Doric Order
          Music
       Junior Warden   (Self)
        Hiram Abiff
        Corinthian Order
        Geometry
      Senior Deacon   (Awakening)
       Composite Order
       Arithmetic
     Junior Deacon   (Feeling)
      Tuscan Order
      Rhetoric
    Inner Guard   (Ego)
     Logic
   Tyler   (Body)
    Grammar

Figure 7

world and like the ego's application of Freud's reality principle, Logic is entirely amoral. Indeed, a skilled debater is expected to be able to apply logical techniques to advocate either side of a proposition without regard for his personal feelings or for the morality of the issue. Thus the Craft depicts the Inner Guard/ego as a level of consciousness which is, at best, capable only of rational activity and like Freud, suggests that morality is resident elsewhere in the psyche. This idea gives us an insight into the cause of the difficulties which beset societies whose members live largely at the level of ego consciousness. It also gives added emphasis to the importance of the Command Relationship between Inner Guard/ego and Junior Warden/Self.

The remaining subject of the Trivium is Rhetoric and is to be associated with the Junior Deacon with whom we have already identified the consciousness level of feeling and intuition. It is the Art by which feeling is introduced into a logical and well structured communication; people are enabled to comprehend through the use of grammatical structure and are instructed by good logic, but they are moved by Rhetoric. As the Junior Deacon is stationed within the Lodge, so feelings and intuition belong to the psyche proper and not to the physical world. They are frequently about the physical world, but they are a purely psychological phenomenon. We saw also that Rhetoric includes formal training of the memory which is not only an exclusively psychological process, but one which relates to a part of the psyche of which one is normally unconscious. The Junior Deacon is the first of the Officers to be associated with an Order of Architecture, which suggests that at this level of consciousness we enter the psyche proper, the area with which Vitruvius deals when he writes of Architecture in a philosophical sense. This is the interior temple of the psyche; and the Tuscan Order, which is the simplest and least refined, indicates that the Junior Deacon/feelings represents the crudest and least sophisticated level of purely psychological activity.

We have associated the Senior Deacon with a level of consciousness which we have called awakening, a state of acute alertness to events which are occurring around the individual and within his lower psyche. Arithmetic, the first of the Sciences, is related to the Senior Deacon. The subject deals with the properties of numbers and the relationships between them and, although it has myriad practical applications, arithmetic itself is entirely abstract with no relationship to the physical world. As a practice it provides training in the precise manipulation of abstract ideas, and it has been used since the time of Pythagoras to convey philosophical concepts. It is a prerequisite for the other sciences which follow in the curriculum in the same way that a capacity for abstraction and an ability to be 'awake' are required for progress in the interior work. While Arithmetic points out the abstract aspects of the level of Awakening, the Composite Order reflects the practical ones. The Composite column combines, in a single capital, the features of all the other orders, and is thus the most complicated of the five. In a similar way the individual who is awake is aware of a vast complex of considerations and ramifications which enable him to recognise that the seemingly separate phenomena of the physical world are, in fact, interacting parts of a single system. Indeed, this is one of the pitfalls of the Awakening state because the integrated view of the world is sometimes so breathtaking that it is mistaken (by credulous candidates) for Illumination. The difference is that Illumination is a lasting condition, while the ecstacy of Awakening soon fades and leaves the candidate with an opportunity to practise perseverance.

Before moving on to a consideration of the levels of consciousness represented by the Principal Officers we should note one more point about those represented by the Deacons. We have said that feeling and awakening are 'purely psychological' levels of awareness and have based this idea on two symbols: the fact that the Deacons are positioned within the Lodge, and that each is associated with an Order of Architecture from Vitruvius' interior model. It is significant that the Orders of Architecture belonging to the Deacons are the Roman Orders, which are considered to be the lesser of the five, and that the Deacons' place is on the Ground Floor within the Lodge. These two points suggest that although feeling and awakening are purely psychological levels of awareness, they are very much involved with the interface between psyche and body and with the individual's ability to operate in the physical world.

With the Junior Warden we begin to consider a part of the psyche which is quite different from that represented by the Assistant Officers, and this difference is indicated by the fact that the Junior Warden and his colleagues are associated with the characters in the Hiramic Legend. Without anticipating our analysis of that story we can observe here that the staircase symbolism associates Hiram Abiff with the Junior Warden, the level of consciousness which we have called the Self. As the Junior Grand Warden at the building of Solomon's Temple, Hiram Abiff was responsible for the actual day-to-day accomplishment of the work. It is from this role and from the association of the Junior Warden with the

First Degree, that we derive the idea of the Junior Warden/Self as the immediate director of that part of the psyche which is in contact with the physical world and through which we accomplish the purpose for which we incarnate. The identification of Hiram Abiff with the Junior Warden suggests that one who is 'self conscious' knows who he is, what he is here to do and how to go about doing it properly. These are qualities which make the Junior Warden/Self an excellent commander for the Inner Guard/ego.

The assignment of Geometry to the Junior Warden's step emphasises the distinction between the principal and assistant Officers. We have devoted a substantial amount of attention to Geometry, and we have seen how it defines the cosmology upon which the Craft's symbolism rests. We need not repeat the details of the cosmology here, but only recognise that at the level symbolised by the Junior Warden one's perspective shifts from a purely individiual view to a perspective with which one can be consciously aware of one's place in the cosmos which Geometry describes. As the picture of the relative universe shown in Figure 5 indicates, the Junior Warden/Self is located at the meeting place of the three lower worlds, and is thus in command of his physical being, at the centre of his psyche and in contact with his spirit. It is this unique location in consciousness which gives the Junior Warden/Self the remarkable capacities ascribed to Hiram Abiff. We can look at the Junior Warden from a third perspective; from the point of view of the Spark of individual consciousness, which originates in Divinity and makes its way through the four worlds into manifestation. In the context of this journey the Junior Warden/Self is the farthest point of progress before the individual incarnates. It is the 'reflection of the reflection' of its Divine source, and it contains within itself all that it has acquired during its journey toward manifestation. In this sense it is like the Corinthian Column which, being the most recent and most refined of the Greek Orders, represents the culmination and farthest development of the Greek Architectural tradition.

The Senior Warden presides over the Middle Chamber, the Soul of the individual. Hiram, King of Tyre is the legendary character associated with the Senior Warden/Soul and, at first glance, it seems a strange connection. The Hiramic Legend does not have a great deal to say about this personage beyond the fact that he was Senior Grand Warden at the building of the Temple, that he was King of Tyre, and that he provided the materials and the labour for the project. Since Tyre was a vigorous and successful commercial port, King Hiram appears to have been very much an influential man of the world, and it is that which makes his connection with the Soul seem unusual. We must remember, however, which world we are talking about. Solomon's Temple, in the sense that we are considering it here, is a building which exists in the psychological world; and that is the context in which King Hiram must be evaluated. Thus the staircase symbolism pictures the Senior Warden/Soul as a highly competent ruler of the psyche, and our notion of the Soul as the central essence of the psychological organism is derived from this image. From Hiram's role in the legend we may infer that one who is conscious at the level of the Senior Warden/Soul has control over the resources of the psyche (the materials of the Temple) and over the psychological vehicle which the individual occupies while operating in the World of Forms. This makes the Senior Warden/Soul responsible for the proper operation of the psyche as a whole and that brings us to the Science of Music. From the perspective of the winding stairs, Music has little to do with the business of playing upon instruments which is, in any case, an Art. The Science of Music is concerned with music theory upon which whole metaphysical systems have been based, as a glance at Robert Fludd's work will show. Among other ideas, he uses the concept of resonance between the same notes in different octaves as an analogy of interaction between corresponding parts of the four worlds. Harmony is a subject which occupies a prominent place in music theory. It deals with the relationships between the several components which make up the musical structure, and by associating it with the Senior Warden/Soul we infer that the Soul's functions include maintaining a harmonious relationship between the components of the psyche. An interesting parallel between the physical and psychological worlds suggests itself. In the physical body the metabolism regulates the balance between the anabolic and katabolic processes which store energy in tissue or break down tissue to produce energy in order that the organism can operate satisfactorily in its environment. Similarly, the Soul regulates the balance between the disciplinary or judgmental and the merciful or forgiving psychological processes in order to keep the psychological organism operating properly. Here, for the first time, we encounter emotion which is a phenomenon of the Soul (in contrast to the feelings of the ego); and we will consider it in greater detail in connection with Labour in the Second Degree. The last insight which the Staircase provides into the nature of the Soul is by reference to the Doric Order. It is the oldest and simplest of the Greek Orders, and there is a certain austerity about it which communicates two ideas. The first is the concept of the Senior Warden/Soul as the paymaster. It is a role which derives from the task of maintaining harmonious relationships, but which also has its sombre side because the Senior Warden pays exactly the wages that have been earned. We will look more closely at this concept in due course. The second idea is that of duration. The Soul and the individual to whom it belongs are things which endure and the age of the Doric Order conveys the notion that the Soul existed prior to the individual's birth into the physical world and will continue to exist after his passing out of it.

The Worshipful Master is the most senior officer of the Lodge. We have seen how he represents that part of the psyche which is closely associated with the world of Spirit, just as the Junior Warden is closely involved with the physical world. As Figure 5 suggests, the Master is also able to perceive the very least part of Divinity. Our interpretation of the Winding Stairs provides three more perspectives to assist us in understanding this level of consciousness which resides within each human being, but which is experienced only rarely. Solomon, King of Israel, conceived the idea to build the Temple. While the other two Grand Officers facilitated the project or accomplished the work, it was Solomon who saw the opportunity and comprehended the purpose of the undertaking. There is a world of difference between the level of competence of the two Grand Masters who read the plans and constructed the building and that of Solomon, who understands the Grand Design (or at least the part of it involving him) and acts, as a free agent, to bring his part of the Design to fruition. This difference in competence gives us a clue about the difference between the Psychological and Spiritual Worlds. The psychological perspective is orientated toward the individual; the spiritual perspective, while recognising the individual and acknowledging his value, at the same time transcends the personal view and understands the individual as being an essential part of the Grand Design. As we have seen, the Tracing Board, the Immovable Jewel associated with the Master, reflects this idea. It is an instrument of design which relates not to individual stones, but to the whole structure containing many stones properly related. The science of astronomy (or more properly, astrology) is assigned to the step of the Worshipful Master/Spirit and the association extends the idea of a transcendent perspective introduced above. While it has become a commonplace to say that the observation of the Heavens gives one an appreciation of the Majesty of Divinity, it is none the less true that contemplation of the night sky can give one a glimpse of the feeling of awe which is one characteristic of contact with one's Spirit (in fact, the relationship between the Junior Warden/Self and the Worshipful Master/Spirit is called the Path of Awe in some traditions). From the Astrological perspective, which is the one likely to have been taken by the Craft's founders, the study of the Heavens enables one to obtain an insight into the Divine Plan. Whether or not one can legitimately interpret astrological data in that fashion is an open question today. However, the Mason who practises his Craft from the point of view we are considering here would do well to accept Isaac Newton's advice and make a thorough, open-minded study of the subject before formulating an opinion. The legitimacy of Astrology notwithstanding, from the point of view of interpretating the staircase symbolism, the intention is quite clear; the level of consciousness represented by the Worshipful Master/Spirit has access to a view of the Grand Design. The Worshipful Master is also identified with the Ionic Order of Architecture. The Ionic Order is in many ways a middle ground. The capital is a symmetrical balance betwen two decorative volutes. These can be thought of as representing the source of the active and passive principles which are integrated at the level of the spirit. The overall Ionic style incorporates the strength of the Doric Order without its bluntness and the grace of the Corinthian Order, without its exuberance. This balanced integration of architectural qualities reflects the integration of the components of the psyche which occurs for one who is conscious at the level of the Worshipful Master/Spirit.

These comments on the staircase symbolism are quite inadequate as descriptions of levels of consciousness. If the descriptions of the Guards seem more 'realistic' and 'precise' than those of the Principal Officers, that is because the Guards' levels of consciousness are familiar in our common experience. In a very real sense one cannot describe a level of consciousness at all; the thing must be experienced to be comprehended. In one way of thinking, the very purpose of Masonic Labour is to climb this staircase of consciousness and the purpose of the symbols is to give a clue about the experience at each step. With this in mind we can turn again to the Second Tracing Board itself, and consider other symbols which give an insight into the dynamics of the psyche at this level and will assist us in our ascent.

The Two Pillars

The Two Pillars which flank both the entrance to the Temple and the

Winding Staircase are among the most prominent symbols in the Craft. They have attracted a great deal of attention, and a wide variety of meanings have been attached to them. The scope of our interpretation is limited by our consideration of the Second Degree Tracing Board as a detailed drawing of part of the First Degree Board; specifically the Point-within-a-circle-bounded-by-two-parallel-lines, the Ladder, and the Glory. If the Winding Staircase corresponds to the Ladder, the Master's Column of Consciousness; then the Two Pillars must correspond to the Two Parallel Lines, the Warden's Columns. The Second Degree Lecture defines the details of these pillars which, taken together, are said to form a stable structure and we must take note of some of these particular characteristics.

First, the pillars appear in the Second Degree; so, while the Apprentice has been introduced to them, we can infer that their detailed consideration at this stage relates to some process which occurs in an area of the psyche beyond the threshold of ordinary consciousness. Second, they are a complementary pair. The Lecture associates them with the Pillars of Cloud and Fire, their adornments are celestial and terrestrial, as the parallel lines they are Moses, the prophet, and Solomon, the Lawgiver, or alternatively the Saints John, whose respective days are midsummer and midwinter. Lastly, of course, their names are opposite. These are the complementary active and passive paired functions we have met before. When balanced by consciousness, it is these functions which form a stable structure by facilitating the operation of the Rule of Three. Third, these pillars are of brass and cast in clay ground outside the Temple. This characteristic should arrest our attention. Since the ritual was at such pains to exclude metal in the First Degree, we might be surprised to find such prominent metallic structures associated with the Second. This metallic quality of the Pillars suggests that whatever unconscious processes are to be associated with them also relate to events which occur – or have occurred – in the physical world. Finally, the pillars are formed hollow to serve as archives. Now, an archive is a place wherein one stores records of historical events. When regarding the Temple as a representation of the individual's psyche we can consider these pillars, the archives, to be his memory, or more properly the part of his individual unconscious where his memories are stored. Most of one's memories are unconscious at any one time, only a part of them can be recalled at will (which is why the columns are so far beyond the threshold of consciousness), and taken as a whole, they comprise an historical record of the individual's experience. In order to understand better the processes which occur during Labour in the Second Degree it will be worth looking briefly at how that historical record is built up and the effect contemporary psychology considers it to have on our psychological behaviour.

Both the Freudian and Jungian schools subscribe to the view that each child receives large quantities of information and experience during his formative years. This material may be processed consciously by the ego (Inner Guard) or assimilated directly, below the limit of his perception. In addition, the child may or may not understand correctly those experiences of which he is conscious, but all of this material passes into his memory where it sinks into the unconscious and is, in general, forgotten. It does continue to remain in the psyche, however, as the remarkable capacity to recall information under hypnosis indicates. In terms of the symbol we are developing here, these perceptions and experiences are stored in the two pillars; material which tends to constrain us in the passive pillar, and that which tends to make us come alive in the active pillar.

The Jungian school takes the view that this stored experiential material is held at the level of the personal unconscious to form emotional associations of related events, some stimulating and some restrictive. These active and passive emotions cluster around various archetypes to form emotional complexes which exert a profound, but unconscious, influence on the behaviour of the individual. Because these associations are usually quite complicated and subtle, their influence may not be at all obvious. Thus, to invent a simplified example, a person who witnessed and repressed a horrific automobile accident during his childhood may not simply have an unexplained aversion to cars, he may also be unable to tolerate milk products because he happened to be eating an ice cream at the time of the event and the food became part of the network of associations related to the experience. The Jungian view of the unconscious influence goes farther than individual experience. It postulates a collective consciousness which is the basis of individual active and passive complexes derived from the individual's cultural beliefs. For example, an individual born into the western democracies will have a deep-seated conviction that all people should be equal before the law and this culturally inherited concept will, on occasion, spur him to vigorous action. Similarly, a person with a strong Roman Catholic cultural background will respond to the concept that remarriage after a divorce is a sin, and his behaviour will be restrained by this belief. It would appear that some concepts, such as a revulsion against incest, are common to almost all humanity.

To the Jungian, these emotional and intellectual complexes within the individual and collective unconscious are highly inter-related and together they form a set of unconscious boundaries and compulsions which define the limits of the behaviour of the individual. In considering the two columns as the repositories of these complexes, it is tempting to think that the shaft of the column holds the emotional (individual) complexes; the Chapiters and Spheres hold the intellectual (collective) complexes; while the network represents the inter-relationship among the associations. The founders of our Craft will certainly not have had Jung's work in mind, but they might easily have observed the same phenomena that Jung describes.

The Freudian school, which is inclined to be more materialistic, takes the position that all the material in the unconscious enters through the senses either consciously or subliminally. According to this view, the experiences of childhood which relate to rewards and punishments serve to define what persons in authority (particularly parents) say the child ought and ought not to do. Those experiences which tend to be restrictive and disciplinary are organised in the unconscious to become the conscience (stored in the passive pillar), while experiences which encourage and reward a specific kind of behaviour combine to form the ego ideal (stored in the active pillar). It is these, taken together as the super-ego, which define the limits of individual behaviour in the Freudian view. While there are substantial differences between these two contemporary views of the unconscious, both are agreed that it contains a large amount of material which originates in the physical world and which exerts a profound and unsuspected influence on the behaviour of the individual. Indeed, the function of the super-ego (or of the active and passive complexes) is to enable the individual to adjust his behaviour in order to fit into his tribe or society. In viewing the two pillars as the memory/personal unconscious, the Craft's model of the psyche agrees with these two contemporary views as far as they go. It is the business of the Fellowcraft Freemason to go farther.

The association of the Pillars with the Staircase in the Second Degree suggests that as the candidate moves from the Ground Floor and begins to operate at the levels of the Junior and Senior Wardens (the Self and the Soul) he has access to the archives of his Lodge, the contents of his personal unconscious. In psychological terms, the emotional and intellectual complexes (Jung) or the super-ego (Freud) which define the nature and limits of his behaviour become available for examination by his conscious awareness. As this happens he comes slowly to understand why he behaves as he does and to realise that his standards of behaviour have been based on rules established outside himself; rules which are quite arbitrary, quite local and quite changeable. The essentially local and artificial nature of the super-ego's morality is described succinctly in the play *The Teahouse of the August Moon*, by the American author, John Patrick. Sakini, the Okinawan interpreter, who is trying to understand the ways of the Americans who have recently occupied his island, says:

> 'In Okinawa...wash self in public bath with nude lady quite proper,
> Picture of nude lady in private home quite improper.
> In America ... statue of nude lady in park win prize;
> But nude lady in flesh in park win penalty.
> Conclusion?
> Pornography question of geography'.

The person who examines the interior reasons for his behaviour also begins to recognise that under some circumstances it might be better if he behaved differently. We have seen that the purpose of the super-ego is to enable the individual to fit into his society. As the Fellowcraft begins to have access to the material stored in the two pillars, that is the experiences which form his super-ego or his emotional and intellectual complexes, he comes to realise that the literal interpretation which his unconscious places upon this stored-up experience may not always produce the best result or generate the wisest counsel to govern his behaviour. He then begins to analyse the requirements of his society and to choose to comply with them when it is appropriate; but now he can also choose not to comply, or to comply in some new and original way, when the circumstances require it. Such a person becomes more of an individual, more in possession of himself, and is in a position to be more understanding and tolerant of others. The individual who has reached this stage is at the point of a very profound change. His situation in the past has been rather like that of a navigator who is guiding his ship down a well-known coast. He shapes his course by reference to the familiar landmarks which appear as the voyage progresses. There comes a time, however, when the ship's destination requires that it venture out of sight of land and at that point the navigator must cease to depend upon external references and must shape his course solely by reference to instruments carried within the ship. This is the point at which the Fellowcraft finds himself. Heretofore, he has made his judgments of right and wrong on the basis of the rules of his society. Now he finds that he can judge right and wrong for himself and that frequently he must do so. When he was an Apprentice, Providence placed him in positions in which he could learn to control the functions of his lower nature. Now, Providence acts to place him in situations in which the conventionally correct answer is not good enough. In these situations, the essentially external references provided by the super-ego offer solutions which are acceptable to the world at large but which the individual knows to be of questionable morality. Alternatively, they may offer no help at all. In either case, the maturing Fellowcraft knows that some internal reference is required which defines the truly correct course of action in the situations in which he now finds himself.

The Craft represents this internal moral reference by the three Working Tools of the Second Degree and labour in this degree consists, in large measure, of recognising the influence of the quite arbitrary rules of his super-ego (or the compulsions of his complexes) and replacing them with those absolute standards of morality which he finds to be within his Middle Chamber, that is his Soul.

5 THE WORK OF THE FELLOWCRAFT

Working Tools

The Working Tools of a Fellowcraft Freemason are the Plumb, the Level and the Square. The essential characteristic of these tools is that each measures against an absolute criterion. As the tools of the Second Degree, they are found in the Middle Chamber, in the individual's Soul. They are well beyond the threshold of ordinary consciousness and they are provided to enable the person who works at this level to define his morality when the ordinary rules of social conduct fail to provide a satisfactory definition. Up until this point we have been considering that part of the Craft's system which is parallelled by contemporary psychology. We have seen that the two approaches have been in some ways similar and, to that extent, psychological concepts have been helpful in interpreting the Craft's symbolism. When he works as a Fellowcraft, however, the individual starts a process which begins to depart from the precepts of conventional psychology (or at least of Freudian psychology) and it is worth observing how this divergence takes place.

We have noted the contemporary views which hold that an individual begins life with a blank, or empty, or unformed psyche and that the experiences of growing up are instrumental in the formation of the ego, the executive of the psyche, and of the super-ego, the residence of the individual's morality. These two structures, together with the id which contains the drives and instincts, are taken by the Freudian to comprise the totality of the psyche. This concept of psychological development is the result of a large body of research, which is based upon the assumption that the entire human being comes into existence at birth (or possibly at conception). Since the Craft's symbolic structure (in common with most institutions which are orientated toward Deity) implies the premise that an individual's Soul, Spirit and Divine connection exist in the upper worlds prior to his incarnation, the Craft tends to put a different construction on the evidence derived from psychological research. The developmental processes recognised by contemporary psychology certainly occur, but in the Craft's model they are concerned specifically with that part of the psyche which integrates the incarnating individual to his physical body and to the physical world. In the Craft's symbolic terms, early psychological development refers to the Ground Floor of the Temple, and to that part of the side pillars which contain the super-ego. In fact, the Craft's recognition of this early development is reflected in the symbolic requirement that one must be of mature age to join the Order, which implies that this process of initial development must be complete before the Craft's work can begin.

Masonic Labour starts, as we have seen, on the Ground Floor and its purpose is to bring that part of the psyche which is closely associated with the body under conscious control. But, as contemporary psychology points out, the psychological organism which develops during childhood is orientated outwardly, its structure is designed to relate to society; it is not orientated toward the Soul and Spirit which incarnated in the first place. Indeed, from the point of view of consciousness, it overlays and obscures the individual's Soul and Spirit. Thus, the labour of the Fellowcraft is intended to bring the faculties of the Soul into consciousness so that the individual human being can emerge and start to live his own life. Like all Masonic Labour, that of the Fellowcraft is accomplished by the use of Working Tools, and in the Second Degree those tools describe functions and qualities which are part of the psyche itself, the Soul which existed before incarnation. The labour of the Second Degree is involved, first with identifying the psychological functions described by the Working Tools and separating them from the super-ego which overlays them, and, second, with learning when and how to use these new standards of morality. People who have accomplished this are relatively rare. When they appear they stand out with great prominence because they transcend ordinary social attitudes. They possess a fundamental morality which cannot be denied, and in their presence the conventional 'right' attitudes are frequently seen to be mere prejudice. Mahatma Gandhi was such a person whose essential moral correctness engendered widespread respect because it cut cleanly through the conventional regulations of the time. It is to this higher concept of morality that the Labour in the Second Degree relates. In our consideration of the subject we will look first at the Working Tools and the qualities they symbolise, and then at some examples in the lives of quite ordinary people which illustrate the labour which employs them.

There are three tools and, as in the First Degree, their employment is an application of the Rule of Three which pervades the Craft's work. The difference in this case is that the active, passive and co-ordinating functions are those of emotion and morality rather than of doing and feeling. The Plumb-rule measures against the absolute standard 'vertical' and this upright orientation associates it with the active functions of emotion and morality. These are sometimes referred to collectively as 'Mercy', but a single word is inadequate to summarise the Plumb-rule's functions which include loving kindness, generosity, benevolence, giving, forgiving, license, liberty, permissiveness, affection and numerous other qualities which relate to the kind, loving, outgoing, unrestrained emotions. Mythology may help us here. The god who represented all these qualities was Jove/Jupiter, whose kingly generosity bestowed largesse on all who came to his attention and whose magnificence destroyed his mortal mistress when it shone on her with full force. These are functions which are generally associated with the ego ideal, but note that the Plumb-rule measures 'vertical' which (like Mercy) is an absolute concept whereas the merciful, rewarding criteria of the ego ideal are simply rules which vary from epoch to epoch and culture to culture.

In a similar way the Level measures against the absolute standard 'horizontal' and its supine orientation associates it with the passive emotional and moral functions. The collective term sometimes used here is 'Judgment' but in this case also, a single word is inadequate to summarise the Level's functions which include discipline, restraint, rigour, containment, circumspection, asceticism, austerity, righteous anger, just punishment, discrimination and all the other emotional and moral functions which tend to hold and restrict. In mythology these qualities were represented by the god Mars, who was not (as he is often pictured today) an untrammelled warrior, but small and dark, the restrained, disciplined defender acting only under orders. These are the conventional functions of the conscience, but again, the criteria for the conscience's restraint is simply a collection of rules, which are the product of an era and a society, while the Level measures against the absolute standard of 'horizontal', of Justice.

There is an important characteristic to notice about these tools, because it reflects a characteristic of the psychological functions they represent; the Plumb-rule always measures vertical, and never measures anything else; and the Level always measures horizontal. In a similar way Mercy is always only merciful, and Judgment is always only just. This is an important point because as one gets control of the psychological functions which the tools represent, one really does have access to absolute Mercy and Judgment; and 'absolute' is a frightening thing. It should be clear that either of these principles, operating alone, would be intolerable. Boundless largesse, unrestrained mercy and the absolute witholding of discipline are gifts which are seriously debilitating to the recipient, as certain attitudes toward child rearing consistently demonstrate. On the other hand, merciless judgment which administers unswerving justice to enforce inflexible discipline has been shown to be an equally destructive regime. The Fellowcraft who starts to come to grips with these tools, in fact, needs desperately to apply the Rule of Three which is facilitated in this case by the Square.

The obvious thing about the Square, or angle of ninety degrees, is that it defines the relationship between vertical and horizontal, between the Plumb-rule and the Level. In a similar way, the quality of the psyche which is represented by the Square must do just that: define the proper relationship in the application of the two psychological functions of Justice and Mercy. Here is the Square in the form essential to the Fellowcraft, a symbol of the absolute standard, 'Truth', and it is used to define the balance between the other tools. This co-ordination or balancing process, symbolised by the Square as a Second Degree Working Tool, is an activity of consciousness at the level of the Soul; and developing this conscious skill is one of the purposes of Labour in the Second Degree. Like the Apprentice, the Fellowcraft usually comes to the work with one tool better developed than the other, or he finds that he has access to one of the tools before the other(s) are available to him. Either case tends to produce an unbalanced situation, and Providence arranges circumstances which will foster the development of the under-developed function, as the following example illustrates.

Consider the situation of a woman, born shortly after the Second World War. As she became a young adult, the permissive attitudes of the mid-1960s fitted very well with her naturally open and giving nature, and she lived for several years in an easygoing, open-hearted life-style. As she matured, she continued in her outgoing pattern of giving. She gave of herself without restraint, in her work, in her charity and in her romantic relationships. Slowly, she realised that, although she was giving and giving, it was not bringing her happiness, or fulfilment, or even close friends. Her world was populated by people who were willing to take, but quite unprepared to make a serious commitment to someone who thrust things upon them incessantly. From the point of view of the tools she had a well-developed Plumb-rule, a very weak Level and a poor concept of the use of the Square. Finally, Providence placed her in a job which demanded that she face the problem of developing her disciplinary and judgmental faculties. Since she was an intelligent woman, she found herself managing a small firm whose business was to provide services to charitable institutions. Working closely with charities was congenial with her generous and giving nature; and she derived great satisfaction from the job, although she did find it worrying that the firm was steadily losing money. One afternoon, upon returning from a delightful business lunch with the representative of an affluent and prestigious charity she realised that she had agreed to provide to the charity access – without cost – to a substantial amount of expensive research. Reflecting on the fact that the particular charity in question could easily afford the fees involved, she realised that she had given the material away simply because it made her feel good. When she made a review of her activities over the previous months, she realised to her horror that she was destroying her company and wasting the resource of its owners simply for the sake of her super-ego's belief that work for gain was wrong, and giving was equated with loving. The shock that came with this recognition was sufficient to cause her to reassess her concept of morality (and to call in the firm's chartered accountant who installed appropriate management controls in the company). At the same time her recognition of her own moral irresponsibility in the situation enabled her to exercise disciplines within herself. Both sets of controls are examples of the use of the Square, in

Masonic terms; and with the guidance of her accountant and the support of her friends, she was able to get both her firm and her personal life operating on a viable basis. She continues to view commercial enterprise with distaste when it exhibits the characteristics of greed, but now she also recognises that an honest entrepreneur is entitled to a good return. Her super-ego's harsh condemnation of business has been tempered by the conscious use of her Level on herself.

The opposite problem was experienced by an army officer, a person of great character and finely developed intellect. When he retired from the forces he found his way into a position in an industrial company, and because of his age and maturity quickly moved into a responsible position which had extraordinarily delicate labour relations implications. His own self-discipline and dedication to the department was of great benefit, but he ran his organisation with a strict and unwavering discipline. His management was unquestionably fair, as even the most militant of the work force admitted, but it was so rigid and so uncompromising that he soon found himself at the centre of an industrial dispute. His highly developed Level, which had served him well in the army (and had saved more than a few of his troopers' lives), was not well suited to an industrial relations problem which required the application of a substantial amount of loving kindness. He was, perhaps, less fortunate than the lady with the well developed Plumb-rule because he did not have the shock of finding himself involved in wrongdoing to motivate him to change. Unwilling to modify a lifetime of discipline to match a new situation, he found himself transferred to a dead-end position which ended a promising second career.

As these examples suggest, interior work at the level of the Soul is not easy; it is certainly not the abode of sweetness, love and peace that some popular views of interior development suggest. In simple terms, it is plain hard work and of all the Craft's symbolic references, labour in this sense is perhaps the most descriptive. The process of working through situations such as those described above requires great perseverance as one comes to understand why it is that he considers this to be right and that to be wrong. In this process, however, the real person, the essence of the individual who incarnated, begins to emerge. The fact that such a person has developed a moral sense of his own does not imply that he abandons the ordinary rules of his society. Indeed, he generally becomes a strong supporter of those rules; but he applies them with skill. He notices where they fit, and applies his own criteria when they do not. The essential quality of such a person is that he is in possession of himself.

The quality of self-possession means that the individual is, in large measure, able to choose his course of action and his ability to choose assures him the attention of a certain class of angel. The Craft makes virtually no mention of angelic beings, except in one particular context. When a person reaches the stage symbolised by the Fellowcraft, when he understands his society's rules and recognises his own capacity for morality, when he can choose what course to take, he begins to be of real influence in the world. At that stage he starts to be of interest to those angels whose task it is to make things awkward. The Craft refers to these beings as 'the insidious' and the assiduous Fellowcraft who genuinely works to develop his capacities can be assured that sooner or later, when he expects it the least, he will receive their ministrations. This brings us to the subject of evil.

Evil

In the ordinary way of things, most people do not encounter evil. They experience the effects of evil and suffer a great deal as a result, but real evil implies free choice. That is why the insidious are introduced in the Second Degree. In the everyday view, evil is considered to be a power which opposes good, and the Devil, the principal agent of evil, is understood to be in competition with the Holy One, striving to undo His works and to enslave His followers. This concept of evil is a useful approximation on which to build rules of conduct for ordinary life in the physical world. However, for those involved in trying to understand themselves and their relationship to the universe and Deity, this conventional view raises a problem more serious than any that it answers. The difficulty is that an evil power supposes a power separate from God, whereas we have seen that our cosmology is based on a God without limit who has brought the entire relative universe and all it contains into being by an act of His will. Such a cosmology is incompatible with the existence of a separate power. Indeed, the acknowledgment of an infinite Deity is incompatible with the notion of anything opposing It.

In fact, a careful examination of the Bible (to use the west's most familiar version of the Volume of Sacred Law) suggests a role of evil quite different from the ordinary view and most other scriptures provide a similar content. In the story of Genesis, the archangels and angels had been created and were performing their tasks before mankind appeared on the scene on the sixth day. Now we are told that while the angels and archangels are created beings (that is they have their source in the World of Creation, the Spiritual World), man is of a different nature, having been made 'in the image of God', that is, having his source in the Divine World. When man appeared in creation on the sixth day, the angelic beings were told that Mankind was their superior, being of a different and higher order. This Divine announcement produced a mixed reaction among the angels. The majority, led by Michael, recognised this situation and accepted it. However, about a third did not. This dissident group was led by Lucifer, whose name means 'the Bearer of the Light', and who was, at that time, the most intelligent and high ranking of the created beings. We are told that he could not bring himself to accept the fact that there could be a being superior to himself. As a result of Lucifer's refusal to accept man's position, there ensued the 'War in Heaven' which culminated in the expulsion of Lucifer and the Angels who had sided with him. There is clearly some need to interpret this anthropomorphic imagery which was devised to represent a conflict of principles and ideas (the content of the Heavenly World) to an ancient culture. We can, however, obtain some quite useful information from it. First, Lucifer's enmity is not with Deity, but with man, whom he sees as supplanting him. Second, it appears that the Deity has chosen to make use of Lucifer in his rebellious state. The Book of Job indicates clearly that there remains close communication between Deity and Satan, as Lucifer came to be called in his new role; and it also gives insight into the nature of that role.

Satan, in Hebrew, means 'the Tester' and it is his task, and that of his associates, to travel throughout the Three Worlds of Separation (east and west through all the levels of consciousness) to test the quality of individual human beings and to lead them away from their easterly course, if possible. It is a task for which he is well qualified, first because he was once the highest of created beings and thus knows his way round, and second because of his irreconcilable enmity towards mankind. If we are to believe the Book of Job, the testers are permitted to use all manner of deception and to break every rule except that they may not destroy the individual (although they may lead the individual to destroy himself). It is to the actions of these beings that the Craft refers when it warns against the 'attacks of the insidious' and, although Satan and his associates cause a serious threat to the progress of an individual, they also play a constructive role in the universe, perhaps in spite of their intention.

We saw in the previous section that as an individual grows, in the sense of knowing himself, he is able to choose, he is able to act more freely and to exercise his own will. He is therefore able to exercise progressively more influence in the world, and to do proportionately more damage if he chooses to act with selfish or malicious intent. This ability to do damage is inherent in man's capacity for free will, and if one examines history, one can see, on occasions, the very point at which a central figure chose wrongly, sometimes with the most serious consequences. Napoleon Bonaparte provides an unusually visible example. He embodied, at first, the democratic spirit which was transforming Europe at the end of the eighteenth century, and he had the opportunity to introduce important social and political reform. Indeed, early in his career he was received not as a conqueror, but as a liberator who would establish the new social order throughout the land. However, at the ceremony during which he was being crowned Emperor by the Pope (who had journeyed to Paris for the occasion) he took the crown from the Pope's hands and placed it on his own head. We can see, in this moment, the action of the Tester. Napoleon was a man of great ability who had the opportunity (indeed the task) to bring real peace and unity to Europe which needed it desperately at the time. At the moment of his coronation he transferred his commitment from the service of the Divine purpose to the service of his own ego. This incident with the crown is, of itself, of little consequence; but it reveals the change in Napoleon's psychological motivation, the erosion of his personal integrity. Napoleon's temptation and the resulting loss of integrity, which gave Europe decades of war instead of the promised social and political reform, is an example of the operation of the Lucific principle, an 'attack of the insidious'.

It is instructive to consider the 'testing by the Wardens' in this context. That important aspect of the First and Second Degree Ceremonies, in which the Wardens 'examine the work' of the candidate, represents a process which occurs within the psyche of the individual and which involves only the various components of the individual's own psychological being. As the individual grows and develops his increased capacities, the Wardens, representing his Self and his Soul – the seat of his morality – examine the way in which he uses these abilities, and approve or criticise. This is the activity of a mature conscience. As long as the individual keeps himself within the limits established by his Wardens he will have little difficulty. He will experience temptation, to be sure; the insidious are an 'external agency' whose job it is to test the quality of individuals. However, a person who has encouraged an internal stability by keeping within the bounds of his own conscience will be prepared to meet these tests when they come. It is the person who has ignored the critique of the Wardens in their testing capacities that is most susceptible to temptation, most likely to sin.

Sin is a concept which is understood differently by different people. Almost all agree that it is bad; but its impact on the individual, its long-term implications, and the remedies appropriate to mitigate its effects are the concerns of an individual's religion and quite outside the purview of the Craft. From the more limited perspective of our present interpretation the effect of sin is to retard, or block, the individual's progress in coming to understand himself. The word means 'to miss the mark' and it is, in this limited sense, an error. There are a great variety of errors, but we can usefully think of them as each being a misapplication of some perfectly proper activity. We can associate a sin with each of the Officers of the Lodge and with each of the Working Tools. It is a useful concept because, if we do find ourselves in difficulty, it helps in the understanding of the problem. For example, the Tyler gone wrong fails to check the intake at the physical level; either he admits improper material or an excessive amount. The Tyler's sin is Gluttony. If the Deacons or Inner Guard should fail, they report inaccurate information or carry erroneous messages; the sin is False Witness. The obvious misapplication of the Gavel or the creative, passionate side of one's nature is Lust; while the improper use of one's analytical faculty, or Chisel, results in Sloth. When we look at the Second Degree's tools we find that one relates to the faculty of judgment and discipline, and its associated sin is Anger. The complementary tool relates to kindness and generosity and when used wrongly its sin is Malice. Every level – even that of the Worshipful Master – has its temptation and corresponding sin (remember that before his fall Lucifer was the highest of created beings). The sin which is usually associated with the three Principal Officers, that is with achievement of some higher level of consciousness, is Pride. These are the 'Seven Deadly Sins' and they are used, in some variation or combination by 'the insidious' to lead the maturing Fellowcraft away from his objective. Like all good quality-control engineers, the insidious direct their tests at the most vulnerable and least well controlled area of the psyche. Those who fail the test frequently cause substantial damage as they fail, but the long-term effect of the Tester's work is to prevent human beings from growing so rapidly that they acquire capabilities they cannot handle.

As with the situations which develop skill in the use of the Working Tools, the tests come in the context of one's life experiences. It will be instructive to look at a pair of samples which indicate that the tests at this level become quite stringent. Consider the businessman who had done very well when employed as a senior manager, and by means of saving and careful investment had been able to accumulate a substantial sum of money. He also had a strong sense of social responsibility and was severely critical of exploitive business practice. When he felt the moment right, he took early retirement and started a manufacturing business of his own in a provincial city. There was little competition for his products; and because of his charm, ability and considerable reputation, he was immediately able to attract a small customer base which would carry his business comfortably through its first years of modest operation while he established the foundation of a solid concern. At the same time he saw in the enthusiastic consumer response for one of his products the opportunity to make the business grow very rapidly. This opportunity for rapid growth required substantial risk not only to his own capital, but to the financial positions of his other investors, creditors and employees, and to his clients who depended heavily upon his firm for an uninterrupted supply of high-quality products. The growth opportunity also involved stretching the representations about his products to the very limit. None of it was, however, illegal. Within the context of the ordinary rules, the behaviour demanded by the high growth opportunity was acceptable. Faced with this choice of growing slowly, with discipline, responsibility and integrity, or quickly, with abandon and questionable ethics, he chose the latter and more risky route. In the Masonic terminology this test required integrity, the application of the Square. It demanded the discipline of the Level to contain the ambition, expansion and passion of the Plumb and Gavel. In the event, he did not exercise that internal discipline. As the company's situation deteriorated he concerned himself less and less with the questions of morality and social responsibility which had been so important to him previously, and more and more with expedient behaviour. Operating, at last, entirely from the level of the ego, he began to say 'If it's legal, it's all right'. When his business finally failed, he lost his home, his savings, his reputation and the respect of his clients, employees and friends. The essential thing to note in this situation is the opportunity for choice. Businesses fail all the time, but in this situation the opportunity for success by slow, steady growth was almost assured. The test came when the individual chose to embark on the course of action which required behaviour he knew was wrong and of which he had, himself, been critical on previous occasions.

Sometimes, the test is less spectacular. A well-established and fashionable artist was recently approached by a young art student seeking advice about his work. The older woman was shocked by the realisation that the student's talent was greater than her own and more deeply disturbed to realise that she felt threatened by the student's talent. She faced a choice; she could acknowledge the young man's talent and encourage it, or she could criticise harshly in an attempt to destroy the talent which she saw as a threat to herself. This was a test of pride, which she failed when she criticised her student and depreciated his work. Only a few will know, only those friends from whom the student sought to find encouragement. Some are artists themselves who will take note of the event. But, in any case, she will have lost an opportunity to grow herself, and, in some way, she will become smaller. If she persists in such behaviour, she will eventually destroy her reputation, her talent and herself. It may seem that these circumstances are ordinary occurrences which happen to everyone. It is, in some ways, true that they are ordinary events – the curriculum for growth works through the events of the world. The quality which sets both these examples of tests apart from every day life is the fact that the individual had the opportunity to make a moral choice about two actions both of which were 'legal' in the ordinary sense, but one of which was 'wrong'. This is true free will with all its responsibilities, and the ability to exercise it is one of the characteristics of work at the level of the Soul.

6   SECOND DEGREE CONCEPTS

Fate, Destiny and Free Will

In describing the First and Second Degrees, we have frequently referred to Providence which arranges the circumstances of one's life so that one can benefit from the experience and grow into progressively deeper knowledge of one's self. Before we go on to consider the Master Mason's Degree, we will take the time to examine the nature of this agency called Providence which does so much arranging on our behalf and of free will which is one of the priviliges and responsibilities of a real Fellowcraft Freemason. This examination requires us to consider the subjects of fate and destiny.

Fate is a concept which relates to an individual lifetime, and we may think of our fate as being represented by that particular Chequered Pavement which forms the Ground Floor of that particular Lodge which is our own psyche. It is the pattern of easy and difficult experiences which a single individual will encounter in the course of his life. In reality, fate is concerned not so much with specific events as it is with the capabilities of the individual and with the types of experience which are needed to enable him to grow and come into possession of himself. Thus, two people, both good leaders, may need to learn how to be of service to mankind. One may find herself the Mother Superior of an Order of Nursing Sisters which works in the Third World, while the other may be a man who is impelled to abandon a successful business career in New York City in order to manage an organisation raising funds for charity. Each of these individuals will lead very different lives and participate in very different external events, but from the point of view of the individual's own internal development, their two fates will be very similar. Both will learn about the business of service to mankind. The essential thing, from the fatal point of view, is not so much the external events but the internal experience.

An individual's fate is determined by the time and circumstances into which he is born and by the qualities of the various components of his psyche. The exterior, cultural situation will determine the general context, the theatre in which the fate will be played out, while the individual's psychological structure will determine the sort of experience he will encounter and the particular lessons he will have the opportunity to learn. In the Craft's idiom we have seen that the functional components of the psyche are represented by the Working Tools, and they provide us with a means to examine this idea. Consider the analytical faculty, which we have seen represented by the Chisel, as an example. Chisels come in all shapes and sizes to achieve a variety of purposes, some are very fine and sharp, suitable for fine detail carving; a person with such a Chisel will be capable of detailed analysis which differentiates between subtle variants. Another person may have an extremely broad chisel, capable of only the most general analysis, but will have a highly developed Gavel, which makes him capable of passionate artistic creativity. The differences between the tools of which we are speaking now are not related to the process of bringing the psychological functions into balance. Here we are considering the nature of the tools themselves which gives the person – even after he has brought his tools into balance – his unique, individual characteristics.

Those who subscribe to astrology might associate a planet with each Working Tool to gain an insight into their quality, and thus into the quality of a particular fate.

While he cannot change the elements which comprise his fate, the individual can respond to his fate in various ways and these responses will result in very different life experiences. Potentially, one can experience one's fate (or the quality of one's individual life) in four different ways, corresponding to the four levels shown on the First Degree Tracing Board. The particular manner in which one responds to his fate reflects the state of one's interior development and thus includes the effects of one's previous activity. If one lives on the Ground Floor with his attention focussed out into the world, one is carried along with the times and is largely a participant in (some would say 'victim of') what happens to his local society. This is the way most people approach life, and is the reason why fate is commonly thought of in terms of 'Why did this happen to me?' When one starts to take responsibility for one's actions, one begins to see possibilities and opportunities in one's circumstances which are not apparent when one places responsibility elsewhere. At this stage one starts to use one's fate, that is to say, one's psychological capabilities and the opportunities in one's environment, to improve one's personal situation. This sort of work can be external (orientated toward material success in the world) or internal (orientated toward personal growth as we are considering it); but its characteristic is that the individual makes conscious use of his own capacities and the circumstances of his environment. This is conscious co-operation with one's fate. An outward orientation is usually associated with the Senior Deacon (level of awakening), while one who has an inward orientation, as well as being generally awake, may work at the level of the Junior or Senior Warden, the Self or the Soul. Conscious participation in one's fate relates to the middle of the First Degree Board and to the Middle Chamber. When one works at the third level, the Spirit, or Holy of Holies, one begins to use one's fate for a greater purpose than simply his own development. Such a person has a trans-personal perspective which enables him to use his capacities and situation for the benefit of the society. This broadened perspective may refer to his tribe, or his village, or his nation, or the entire human race. The scope of the work done by a person who tries to live his fate at the level of the Spirit is determined by other factors which we will look at in a moment; but the hallmark of a fate which is accepted at the spiritual level is that it transcends individual considerations. Finally, at the fourth level, the person can use his fate, his particular capacities and circumstances, for the conscious service of God. This is one meaning of the Parable of the Talents in the Christian Scripture.

As soon as one begins to co-operate with his fate, and particularly when one starts to use it for purposes beyond his own objectives, one finds that the circumstances of one's fate are uniquely rewarding. As experiences unfold one realises that in the context of each fate there is a particular position, a special role; and to occupy that position and play that role brings one supreme happiness and fulfilment – regardless of the opinion of others. As attractive as such service may sound, co-operation with one's fate should be undertaken with care. It should be clear that there is a close relationship between co-operating with one's fate and accepting responsibility for one's actions. Both these concepts come into sharp focus in the Middle Chamber where our ancient brethren went to receive their wages without scruple or diffidence. There seems to be nothing in the history of the ancient Middle East to suggest any justification for believing in 'the great reliance which [labourers] placed in the integrity of their employers in those days'. This is another bit of the ritual which demands, by its questionable historical accuracy, to be interpreted allegorically. There is, however, a process related to wages which is universally recognised by mankind. Our Buddhist and Hindu colleagues call it Karma; our Christian friends say 'As ye sow, so shall ye reap'; the physical scientist tells us that we cannot get more from a system than we put into it; even the economist recognises it when he says, 'There is no free lunch'. In spite of the fact that many try to avoid the situation or to pretend otherwise, the human race knows very well that 'You get what you deserve'. This is what the Craft is referring to in its teachings about wages. The Craft's image does make some additional points, however, and they are worth noting. First, the payment takes place in the Middle Chamber, our Soul, which tells us that the paymaster is internal, or at least, he operates through an internal agency. That is why the wages are always paid. Second, 'without scruple or diffidence' means that when the wages come, we know that the wage is what we have earned and that the paymaster is fair. Third, the fact that we go to the Middle Chamber indicates that by the time one begins to work as a Fellowcraft one is conscious of the operation of the payment process. Lastly, although the ritual does not mention it, we should note that honest paymasters are prompt with the wages, and the more senior the workman, the more prompt is the payment. The operation of this last principle may not be immediately apparent to the Fellowcraft who is doing nicely and is entitled to enjoy the benefit of his labour. However, if he should depart from the proper course, ignore his responsibility, or compromise his integrity, his wages will be less enjoyable, and he will realise that by the time that one has become a Fellowcraft and participates actively in one's fate, the payment of wages is exact and immediate. Our eastern brethren call it 'instant karma'.

Destiny is related to fate, but it is of a different order. The notion of a Divine Plan and an ordered creation (such as the one described by the Craft's concept of Geometry) implies purposeful activity throughout the Four Worlds. One's destiny has to do with this Grand Design, not with personal development, but with the purpose for which one was brought into existence. This is a much more profound and far reaching idea than simply birth and the circumstances surrounding one's entry into the physical world. Destiny has to do with the Deity's reasons for creating one's spirit, giving it a soul and causing it to incarnate. Strictly speaking, the subject of destiny is part of the Greater Mysteries which deal with the World of Spirit, and is beyond the scope of the Craft. Still, the work of the Master Mason touches on the edge of this subject and we should understand the concept because as one grasps one's fate and begins to co-operate with it consciously, particularly at the transpersonal level, one begins to fulfil one's destiny.

One must be careful in seeking an example of a man who illustrates this quality because there is a tendency among some to attribute the accolade 'Man of Destiny' to figures of the moment, who turn out, in retrospect, to be quite ordinary. Historical examples are uncommon but not impossible to find. Consider General Douglas MacArthur, who commanded the American forces in the South West Pacific during the Second World War. He was born in the Far East where he acquired an insight into oriental (and particularly Japanese) psychology. His army career was excellent and he retired as a distinguished officer in 1937, prior to the Second World War. Recalled to active duty in 1941, he became famous when he lost the Philippines to the Japanese in 1942. He spent the remainder of the war fighting a low-priority action in Malaysia, much over-shadowed by the naval war in the Pacific. In Korea he was relieved from duty because of his disagreement with President Truman. These circumstances would cause him to be considered a competent, if wilful, professional soldier, and perhaps to be a person who co-operated with his fate. He was, however, the officer who received the Japanese surrender in 1945 and commanded the Army of Occupation in Japan, and in that capacity he performed in a way that has the quality of destiny. In 1945 there was substantial feeling in the United States that the Emperor of Japan should be removed from power; some said he should be executed. General MacArthur recognised what few other American commanders could have understood at the time, that the Emperor was the key to the Japanese nation and its recovery. MacArthur's (often unpopular) decision to recognise the Emperor preserved the Japanese national identity, made possible the nation's reconstruction, and saved the western Pacific from years of chaos and violence which would have resulted if the cohesive force of the Emperor's presence had been removed. It is action of that sort, which affects the lives of millions of people over periods of decades, which has the quality of destiny.

A moment's consideration of the scheme outlined above will bring the realisation that it requires substantial administration. A little reflection on one's own life will make it clear that individual fates are highly interrelated; that while many of one's acquaintances are the result of casual meetings, some meetings which have resulted in important relationships, must surely have been carefully arranged. The administration which sets up and supervises individual fates, manages their inter-relationships, and arranges the opportunities for them to fulfil the plans of destiny is called Providence. It is a function of the World of Creation (the Spirit) and we may infer that Providence, the management of all the fates of all the beings throughout the universe, represents a substantial proportion of the activity of Heaven.

Now, at last, we are in a position to look at free will. One might legitimately feel that with all the providential administration going on in the upper worlds there is very little opportunity for freedom among incarnate human beings. In some respects that is true. Free will is not the licence to do as one chooses; in many ways it is more limited than we are often led to believe. It will be useful for us to start by considering the various impediments to freedom of action which constrain an individual and the things one can do to remove them. First, there are the demands of the body acting through the lower psyche. A person who operates at the physical level is driven by his passions or obsessed by his analytical capacities. While he may protest that it is his own choice to spend his time exclusively in the pursuit of food, drink and/or romantic relationships or in the analysis of the syntax of ancient languages, careful observation of a person who really works from the Ground Floor of his psyche reveals that he is actually unable to behave otherwise. As we have seen, Labour in the First Degree is intended to bring the psychological functions of analysis and passion under conscious control so that one can choose how and when to apply them. By the time one starts to work as a Fellowcraft the seductive beauty or the intriguing idea may arrest one's attention momentarily, but they no longer compel one's behaviour.

The second set of constraints on one's freedom of action are the demands of society. These, as we have seen, are incorporated into one's psychological structure during childhood to form the super-ego, as Freud called it, which influences the individual in such a way that his behaviour matches society's expectations. The labour in the Second Degree brings the compulsions and constraints of the super-ego into consciousness. It enables the individual who works as a Fellowcraft to examine the demands of his super-ego and to decide to follow the socially orthodox behaviour or to adopt some alternative means of satisfying his own and society's requirements.

As these observations indicate, many of the principal impediments to free will are to be found in the individual's own psyche, and a mature Fellowcraft can be seen to be one who has gained control over the functions which can operate in that way. Indeed, such control over one's psychological nature can be considered to be one of the secondary objectives of Masonic Labour in the First and Second Degrees. The remaining factors which limit one's ability to choose and thus to exercise free will, are one's fate and one's destiny; these cannot be brought under one's control in the same way that one's internal capacities can. They certainly exercise a very real limitation on one's activities. For example, the gifted ballerina who dances like a dream but is entirely innumerate will never achieve, by an act of free will, a position of leadership of the Society of Chartered Accountants. Nor will a sedentary holder of such an office, who cannot sense rhythm in a marching band, ever be acclaimed as her partner, no matter how much he wills himself to dance. As we have said, free will, as a philosophical concept, does not imply that everyone is free to do whatever one chooses. Free will is rather a particular attitude towards one's fate; an attitude which looks for and exploits the opportunities that life presents. It means that within the context of one's circumstances, one has choices and one is free to make those choices wisely (that is toward personal and social integration, growth and harmony) or foolishly (toward separation and chaos) as he wishes. This is a doctrine which is foreign to a society which has an ethic of material achievement. And yet, when one gives it a try, when one actually attempts to find one's place in the Grand Design, unexpected opportunities open, improbable rewards appear, and personal fulfilment of a sort not available in the ordinary world comes easily to hand.

Note that the exercise of individual freedom, of what we might call 'my will', is the prerogative of the Fellowcraft. To put it another way, free will is possible only in the Middle Chamber, at the level of the Soul, or Senior Warden. On the Ground Floor, one is influenced by the body and the laws of the Physical World. Only in the Middle Chamber, which is purely in the Psychological World, can one bring together all the components of one's situation, evaluate them and choose freely. It may seem strange that free will is the quality of the Fellowcraft and not the Master Mason. In fact, free will and the maturity and balance which enables one to exercise it are prerequisites for the Ceremony of Raising. The Master Mason, however, works at the level of the Holy of Holies. That level is intimately connected with the spirit and influenced by the laws of that world, as the Ground Floor is influenced by the body and the laws of physicality. The individual's will can no longer be exercised freely under this influence; indeed, in order to gain access to the Holy of Holies in his own Temple the now mature Fellowcraft must surrender his hard won 'my will' to 'Thy will'. That surrender is one of the chief subjects of the Master Mason's Degree.

CHAPTER 5
King Solomon's Porch

1 THE CEREMONY OF RAISING

In the introduction to the Lecture on the Third Degree, we find the statement, 'To a perfect knowledge of this Degree few attain. . .'. It is a humbling idea, not much dwelt upon by those Brethren who do not like to think that their knowledge of the Craft may in some way be incomplete. The statement echoes similar ideas to be found in all mystery systems – 'many are called, but few are chosen' is the Christian idiom; in Greece it was 'the candidates are many, the Initiates few'. It is certainly true that of the many people who start on the path of interior development, on the journey to the east, many get stuck along the way. The reasons should be clear enough from the examples in the previous chapters. The step represented in the Third Degree, however, is an unusually large one. It is, in fact, difficult even to speak about the Ceremony of Raising because, in the same way that the work of the Fellowcraft is generally misunderstood, so the processes of Raising are virtually incomprehensible in terms of everyday human experience in the material world. In this section, even more than in the previous two, we must depend upon the device of interpretating the symbolic structure of the Craft, and we must place our trust on the fact that the individual Mason will, in the course of his travels, come at last to experience this event for himself. In the Second Degree the Work relates to the fourth part of a circle, to a single word. In this Degree the candidate is enabled to 'render the circle of [his] Masonic duties complete'. It is the same circle being referred to, and the man who experiences this Raising in fact, rather than in ceremonial representation, can in truth operate consciously in all four worlds.

When the Candidate for Raising presents himself at the door of a Master Mason's Lodge, he is (according to the symbolism, at least) a very remarkable man. He has brought the ordinary physical and mental processes under control, he has acquired an understanding of his deeper psychological processes, and he has demonstrated his conscience and moral fibre with respect to their use. The fact that he is prepared to forgo the use of these substantial capabilities for his personal benefit is an indication that the candidate has achieved a substantial detachment from the goods and pleasures of the physical world. It seems strange, then, that the password by which he gains admission to a Master Mason's Lodge should be closely related to the substance used to epitomise materiality and the acquisition of physical goods. There are two reasons for this reference to the physical world at this point in the candidate's journey. First, by giving the candidate such a name, the Craft implies that he has become the master of the things symbolised and can use them without becoming 'contaminated' by their influence. A similar concept is to be found in the Christian and Jewish mystical traditions in which the individual had to 'know the angels by name', that is be familiar with and equal to them, before they would let him pass on his journey through Paradise and Heaven. The Chinese picture this state by showing a sage seated backwards on a horse. Here, the notion is that the old man's control of the horse (his body and its psychological environment) is so complete that he can ride safely in this obviously dangerous position. This is the level of detached control which the candidate for the Third Degree is said to have achieved over his lesser nature. The second reason for this reference to things of the physical world has to do with the purpose of creation. In the first section, we saw that the Deity called the relative universe into being so that 'God might behold God' and that the three lower Worlds of Separation were created, formed and made so that Adam Kadmon, the Image of God, might experience all things. As part of this Grand Design, each individual on his journey back to his home in the Divine World carries his fragment of experience, his worldly possessions, which will contribute to the whole experience of the Divine Adam. In this context, the password identifies the candidate as a pilgrim carrying a precious cargo as he starts on this critical phase of his journey.

The candidate enters the Master Mason's Lodge with his eyes open, that is with his physical and mental faculties alert; but he cannot see. In the ordinary interpretation, we say that the darkened Lodge alludes to the darkness of death. In a certain sense, which we will examine in due course, it does. In a more subtle way the darkness implies that the Master Mason's Lodge exists at a level of consciousness not heretofore experienced by the candidate. The 'light' (consciousness) which illuminates this place is of a more subtle nature than that which illuminates the psyche, and the organ of perception within the candidate by which he can respond to this more subtle light is not yet active. Indeed, the Master Mason's Lodge symbolises a consciousness in contact with a different world, the World of the Spirit, and the whole purpose of the Degree is to comment on the nature of the transition between the Worlds of the Psyche and the Spirit. When this transition is complete, and the candidate is able to operate with the consciousness of a Master Mason, the lights in the Lodge are turned on. The candidate should understand this illumination not as a change in his environment, but as the activation of that faculty within himself which enables him to see in the ambient light of a 'Master Mason's Lodge'.

After his admission, the candidate is again the object of a prayer offered for him on his behalf. The prayer, although quite formal, is of great importance because, as we have seen, a properly run Masonic Lodge will never undertake its labour without the consent of the Deity and, in addition, the event of Raising will not occur, in fact, without the influence of Divine Grace. Then follows a series of tests during which the candidate demonstrates his proficiency in the previous Degrees (symbolised by giving the signs) and the fact that he is properly prepared for Raising. These symbolic tests represent events which occur deep in the psyche and which ensure that the individual does not expose himself to the risks of expanded consciousness until he is ready to experience it. In a sense, these testings occur continually in a manner similar to, but more profound than, those which we have observed in connection with the passing from the Degree of Apprentice to Fellowcraft. Until one is ready to pass these tests, one is entirely unaware of them, let alone the responses needed to pass them. When the Lodge (that is, his own interior being) is content that the individual is properly prepared, he is permitted to take the obligation (that is to make the commitment) which sets the process of Raising in motion.

The obligation of a Master Mason is, by far, the most comprehensive commitment required in any of the Three Degrees. Even if it be interpreted in its narrowest, most literal sense, the adherence to the provisions of the obligation is likely to cause a change in one's behaviour. If one interprets it broadly, the obligation effects every department of one's life. In fact, however, a careful examination of the obligation of a Master Mason indicates that, with the exception of summonses from a Master Mason's Lodge and the commitments to secrecy which we will discuss below, the several provisions are a catalogue of the proper relationships between mature human beings, and nothing more. The difference between the (real) Master Mason and other people is that, if one is in conscious contact with the upper part of one's psyche and the contiguous part of one's spirit a conscious departure from these proper relationships will cause serious and immediate damage to the persons involved. Although it stresses relationships with one's brother Master Masons, the fact of the matter is that the obligation applies to all mankind. One should understand this (and all Masonic obligations) in the context of the duties one owes 'to God, one's neighbour and one's self'. Indeed, the candidate for the real (in contrast to the ceremonial) Raising is about to experience an event which will teach the lesson of the brotherhood of man with startling intensity. There is, however, a sense in which the provisions of the obligations do apply particularly to the Brethren and that is in the area of instructing a less experienced brother. This brings us again to the subject of secrecy.

Secrecy in the Master Mason's obligation has two aspects. The first is the same sort of secrecy about the work of the Degree that we have noted in the previous two obligations. At the purely exoteric level this secrecy relates, as we have seen, to the symbolic modes of identification. The actual secrets, that is, the body of information known to people who have become consciously aware of their indwelling spirit by making the transition we are about to consider, cannot be communicated between individuals in any conventional way. We can infer that the obligation requires that the new Master Mason will not improperly induce the experience in others. In any case, the concept (which we saw in the Entered Apprentice Degree) of secrecy as a container for one's experience is as valid and important for the Master Mason as it is for the Apprentice.

The second aspect of secrecy deals with the secrets of a Brother Mason. It is worth noting that, in this respect, the obligation requires one to keep 'his secrets when entrusted to my care – murder, treason, felony, and all other offences contrary to the laws of God and the ordinances of the realm being at all times most especially excepted'. With all those exceptions, one might wonder what sort of thing could be considered a Brother's personal secret. In fact, the reference has to do with the manner in which one works at the business of Masonic Labour as a process of interior development. As one tries to see the Divine laws which are described in the Craft's symbolism operating in one's own life, one begins to understand one's personal experience in a new light. Events from the past, and particularly one's own actions, appear in a new, sometimes painful context. These events are often intensely personal and not infrequently involve deep remorse. The intimate discussions in which these personal experiences are shared and understood in the context of the operation of Divine law result in the sharing of 'a Brother's secrets'. The necessity for secrecy in this context should be obvious and the failure to maintain such secrecy will certainly reduce the effectiveness of a Lodge as a means to assist in individual growth and may destroy it altogether.

The last provision of the obligation which we will consider is the requirement to answer summonses. At the level we are considering, this does not refer to the bit of paper which comes through the post to summon us to the 'duties of the Lodge'. It is much more than that. The sign of a Master Mason, that is the *real* sign, the quality that sets him apart, is in one sense quite obvious to the world at large. Only another (real) Master Mason can recognise the sign for what it is, but its quality shines clearly like a beacon, and almost everyone recognises the person who exhibits it as someone extraordinary. Such a person is recognised as 'one to whom the burdened heart may pour forth its sorrow, to whom the distressed may prefer their suit', although just why this should be, most people would be at a loss to say. But they ask for help. The calls come by letter, telephone or 'out of the air', but they come, and they cannot be ignored. These calls for help form a major part of the 'summonses sent' from a Master Mason's Lodge (even though the person sending may be unaware that such a 'Lodge' exists within him) which one must answer to the limit of his own skill in the Craft.

The traditional penalty of this obligation, like the others in the Craft, is entirely allegorical. It is enough to say that it relates to the centre of one's being. In the ancient times the penalty was used in an attempt to destroy that part of the person which ordinarily survives death. Such an idea is clearly superstitious, but taken as a serious allegory, it gives a clue to the scope of the obligation, and to violate the obligation (in a real sense) is to separate one's self from the possibility of conscious awareness of the Deity.

When the candidate looks at the three Great Lights on which he has been obligated, their configuration indicates that he is in an area of the psyche in which the Spirit predominates. The Lodge is still dark because, although he has assumed the responsibilities, he has yet to experience the transition by which he will be enabled to 'see' in this environment.

2 THE TRADITIONAL HISTORY

The portion of the ceremony of Raising which follows the obligation is deceptively simple. In its exoteric sense it is a beautiful object lesson in fidelity and steadfastness, and most Masons interpret it in that way. In its allegorical interpretation, it appears very quickly to be a teaching of ingenious construction and cosmic scope. The travail and subsequent Raising fill the place in the ceremony which is occupied by the 'testing of the Wardens' in the previous Degrees. In this case, however, the candidate has left behind the levels of consciousness which the Wardens represent. He is about to make a transition into a different world, and his test is the transition itself. The ceremony surrounding the Raising actually deals with two related subjects: the raising of the candidate and the traditional history. We will consider each of these subjects separately in order to catch a glimpse of the purpose of the Degree.

The traditional history describes the murder of one of the chief architects at the building of Solomon's Temple. This crime is said to have taken place at a time when 'the work [on the Temple] was nearly completed', and the unavailability of the architect was such a profound loss that the project could not be completed as it had been planned. Indeed, the ritual suggests a loss of universal scope which requires a temporary arrangement to substitute for the original intention. Note that the traditional history contradicts the Biblical account of Solomon's Temple, which states (I Kings 7:40) that the architects finished all the work they did for Solomon. This apparent contradiction between the Craft's central legend and the Judeo-Christian version of the Volume of Sacred Law, the Craft's most venerated authority, together with the scope of the loss implied indicates that the traditional history has reference to an event very different from the construction of an ancient building. One does not need to look far to find the alternative. There are legends which appear in cultures all over the world describing some primordial tragedy which is the cause of humanity's present situation. Even in the western traditions, the story of this fundamental loss is told in a variety of forms of which our traditional history is but one. Here we will consider this primordial event as it is recorded in the Judeo-Christian idiom where the doctrine is called the Fall of Man.

It is difficult for western man to analyse the fall and expulsion from Eden objectively. From one point of view our culture's materialistic orientation makes light of such 'old fashioned tales' and advises us not to consider them seriously because they have no scientific basis. On the other hand the story of the Fall of Man has been the subject of so much religious commentary, and the concepts of original sin and its associated guilt have become so much a part of collective western thought, that it is difficult to detach one's self in order to study the subject at all. The scientific objection is actually easy to deal with. The reason that the material in Genesis 1 and 2 lacks scientific basis is because it deals largely with a body of human experience which is outside the field properly investigated by the physical sciences. We have seen that the Biblical account of Creation (to use the Judeo-Christian idiom) relates to the creation of the Spiritual World and the formation of the Psychological World; the phenomena investigated by the physical sciences do not appear in Biblical material until after the expulsion of the first human beings from Eden. It is harder to get a grip on the subjective attitudes about original sin which have become accepted unconsciously as part of our western frame of reference. We can get some perspective on the subject, if we try to envisage the process of the Fall of Man in a context which makes use of both the Biblical material and the findings of scientific community. We will develop this idea with the attitude of one who describes an event in the remote past, and our perspective will not be limited to the physical world.

We have already considered the first chapters of Genesis as a description of the creation and formation of the spiritual and psychological worlds, events upon which western science does not comment. The moment of 'Making' corresponds to the 'Big Bang' with which most physical scientists hypothesise that the physical universe began. The development of the physical universe is not discussed in the Biblical account; and we can consider that universe, and our own planet, evolved according to the accepted theories of physical cosmology, geology, biology and evolution. Meanwhile, in the Upper Worlds, human beings were 'called forth, created [and] formed', at which stage they participated in the events described in the stories of Eden. Now the term 'Garden of Eden' has a very exact connotation in the Jewish mystical tradition from which the book of Genesis is derived. It refers specifically to the World of Formation, to the psyche. Thus, we may understand the encounter with Lucifer in the form of a snake to be an event which occurred in the Psychological World and at a time before human beings made their appearance in the physical world. That appearance occurred when the evolutionary processes (operating under divine law) had produced an animal which had a nervous system capable of being a vehicle for human consciousness. At that time the first of the 'men and women' were 'expelled' from Eden, the psyche, and sent into incarnation in the physical world where they occupied the 'coats of skin', the animal bodies, which Divinity had 'made' for them. It has been customary in the west to regard the whole affair as the result of Adam's 'sin', and to think that somehow the business could have been avoided, if only Adam had done as he had been told. On reflection, however, it seems unlikely that an event of such scope and importance as the introduction of human consciousness into the physical world could have been unforeseen by an Agency with the attributes of Divinity. We can suggest that Adam's 'sin' indicated the capacity for free will which is present in human beings. It also involved the acquisition of some awareness of the World of the Spirit, where the paired concepts of Good and Evil first emerge. At this stage Adam, representing mankind, descended into the physical world. It was the process by which consciousness was extended into the most remote part of the relative universe.

In the Craft's Legend, which treats the same event, we find something of the same quality. The architect permits himself to be murdered in the service of some greater cause, and the details of the Legend give us some additional clues into the nature of the Fall. The placement of the Legend in the Third Degree suggests that it is an event which occurred deep in the psyche, in the collective unconscious to borrow Jung's term. This supports the view that we are considering an event which relates to the entire human race. The murder was committed with the working tools of the Fellowcraft, except that the Square of Truth has been replaced by an Apprentice's Tool, the Gavel of Passion in its grossest form. As well as emphasising the psychological nature of the event, the symbolism suggests that the process has to do with the effect of wilfullness and uncontrolled passion where truth and integrity should be found.

The result of the architect's murder was the loss of something of great importance, the Secrets of a Master Mason – that is, the things known to a person who is in contact with the level of the Spirit within himself. The reason that the secrets can no longer be communicated is that the murdered architect, the Junior Grand Warden (representing the Self in this Primordial model) is no longer in his place. Like Adam, expelled from Eden (the psyche) into the physical world and no longer able to converse with Deity, the slain architect (the Self) is said to have been interred (in Earth, the element of the Physical World) in a grave (body) 'five feet or more in depth' (varying with each individual) outside the

Holy of Holies (where Divinity is manifest) and of very limited extent in an east-west direction (the dimension of consciousness). It would appear that the extension of consciousness into incarnation in the physical world involved a disruption in the continuity of consciousness through the Four Worlds. The Craft's symbolism suggests that this loss may be due to the Self being overwhelmed by the passionate nature of the physical vehicle. In any case, this disruption in the continuity of consciousness through the worlds is the loss which the Worshipful Master undertakes to assist in repairing when he opens a Master Mason's Lodge. The extension of consciousness across worlds appears to involve a process which is in some ways analogous to death. Death is the other subject treated in the Ritual of Raising.

3 DEATH

In spite of the meaning conventionally attributed to the ritual, the death which is enacted by the candidate in the Third Degree is quite clearly not the physical death which terminates our period in incarnation, for at its conclusion the ritual includes reuniting the candidate with 'the companions of his former toils'. The ceremony implies an event which is much more profound and very much less frequently experienced than the death of the body. None the less, the act of dying is one of the human processes most commonly used as an allegorical representation of this more profound event which occurs deep within the being of the mature and properly prepared candidate; and an examination of that physical process will serve us as a starting point for our attempt to glimpse the nature of the event itself.

From the clinical point of view, death comes when the biological machinery ceases to operate and the body begins to decompose into its constituent chemicals. From the perspective of a materialistic philosopher, the cessation of body function is the cause of death, and that (apart from the chemistry of decomposition) is all there is to it. The Craft's point of view of death is very different. We have seen throughout that the human being is considered to be a native of the Upper Worlds. He has a soul which acquires a body when it incarnates at moment of birth. The individual human being occupies his body in much the same way that a driver occupies his automobile and the cessation of biological function, rather than being the cause of natural death, is the result of the vacating of the body by its occupant. In our model of the relative universe (Figure 5) there seems to be a definite barrier between each of the Four Worlds. The barrier between the Divine World and the World of Creation is referred to as 'the Abyss' in the description of creation in Genesis 1, and a similar barrier exists at the boundary between the remaining Three Worlds. Birth appears to be a process by which the individual, inhabiting the Psychological World, acquires a vehicle suitable for operation in the Physical World. As the child grows, he develops his ego, which, as we have seen, acts as an agency by which the individual operates across the boundary between the physical and psychological worlds. In the Craft's symbolism, we have seen this boundary represented by the door of the Lodge, and the Inner Guard, who controls the passages across that boundary, is the Craft's representation of the ego's function. In this way we can say that every incarnate human being operates in two worlds, or at least in part of them. Physical death is the individual's transition – in consciousness – back across the barrier between the physical and psychological worlds. In this context, birth and death can be seen as processes by which individuals cross the boundary between the two lowest worlds. Birth is the process of extending the consciousness 'downward' (in Figure 5) into the physical world, and death the process of transition in an 'upward' direction. We can think of incarnate humanity as the agency by which a conscious link across that barrier between the psychological and physical worlds is maintained. To this extent, it would seem that the evolution of mankind has already made some progress in repairing the loss described in the Legend of Creation. We have seen that man is a being which is capable of conscious operation in all Four Worlds; but at the present level of development of human consciousness the majority of mankind bridges the boundary between only the lowest two. The purpose of the transition in the Third Degree is to enable the candidate to penetrate the barrier between the Psychological and Spiritual worlds. It is analogous to the transition ordinarily associated with physical death, but it relates to the next higher boundary, and it is to be accomplished while the candidate remains incarnate. With this concept of birth and death as a 'boundary crossing' activity, we can approach consideration of the allegorical death in the Ceremony of Raising. The newly obligated Master Mason is provided with a brief recapitulation of the first two Degrees. While it is not generally appreciated by the candidate, it puts his position in perspective and it serves as an indicator of the sort of person to whom the event symbolised by the Raising is likely to happen. Starting with the ordinary ego consciousness, he has made contact with his Self, the individual occupying the body. He has brought his passions and analytical capacities of that physical vehicle under control so that it has become a reliable servant. He has brought much of what is generally known as the unconscious into his consciousness and investigated the relationships and interactions between the Psychological and Physical Worlds. He has been tempted to misuse the abilities which this understanding and these investigations have given him, and he has demonstrated his moral soundness by resisting those temptations. In the process, he has developed his own will. It is this man, in control of his psyche and his body and in a large measure understanding the relationship of both to the Divine Plan, who is 'entitled to demand that last and greatest trial'.

It is unnecessary to comment on the details of the ceremony by which the candidate is introduced to the transition process of which death is the allegory, but we can extract some of the principles from it. We have already seen that it is the crossing of a barrier between worlds. We should note that it is not the ego which is slain, that was subjugated long ago. It is the Self, symbolised by the Junior Warden in the Lodge and the Junior Grand Warden in the traditional history, that 'dies'. That Self is the individual, the resident of the Psychological World, who must be true to his principles and surrender his will (which he has worked so hard to attain) to the demands of a greater purpose. Note that in this process the trusted functions of the psyche which have been developed with such care are actually a liability in this situation. This is because the individual, who had once thought of himself as a body and now considers himself to be a psychological being, is about to cross the threshold between the Psychological and Spiritual Worlds. To do so he must die to his concept of himself as a Self (the essence of the psychological organism) in order to realise his identity as a Spiritual being who possesses a Self; just his Self possesses a body. The allegorical death represents the entry into this transition process.

The act of Raising represents the emergence from the transition process into the World of the Spirit. Notice that the two Wardens, both representations of lower parts of the psyche, cannot accomplish this process, but the Worshipful Master, representing that part of the psyche at the level of the Spirit and in contact with Divinity, accomplishes the task with the help of the Wardens. The Lecture on the Third Degree indicates that one is enabled to be raised by 'the help of God [Divinity], the united aid of the Square [Psyche] and Compasses [Spirit] and my own industry [Materiality]', a clear indication in symbolic terms that the process involves activity in all Four Worlds. The Lecture goes on to say that the candidate has been raised 'from a superficial flat to a lively perpendicular'. The reference is to the geometric progression by which the Craft describes the Four Worlds, and shows quite clearly that the candidate is considered to have crossed the barrier between the 'superficies' of the psyche and the 'line' of the spirit.

The posture into which the candidate is raised is of great importance. It is a symbol of the oneness which pervades the relative universe. Heretofore, it has been one of the fundamental principles upon which the Craftsman has based his work; now it is a conscious experience. At this point in the ceremony the lights in the Lodge room are turned on, indicating to the candidate that his transition is complete and that he is now able to see in the ambient light of a Master Mason's Lodge. It is by this light that he will perform his Labours in the Third Degree.

4 THE WORK OF A MASTER MASON

The Ritual and Lectures do not have a great deal to say about the labour of a Master Mason. The Charge urges the newly raised Master Mason to give his attention to 'that most interesting of all human studies, the knowledge of yourself', and suggests that he get on with it while he can. The Lecture indicates that Master Masons are the preservers of the Ancient Landmarks of the Order, and the source of instructors and Rulers of the Craft. Beyond these general comments, however, very little is said about the actual work of a Master Mason. Considering the awesome scope of the experience represented by the Ceremony of Raising, it is small wonder that little is said about labour in the Third Degree. In fact, the nature of the work is such that very little can be framed into words. The examination which we will make must rely heavily on the interpretation of the Craft's symbolism in order to comment on the subject at all.

Of the Immovable Jewels, the Tracing Board is said to be for the Master to 'draw designs on', and this image contains two powerful ideas. First, unlike the First and Second Degrees which are concerned with the shaping and trying of an individual stone, the Third Degree is concerned with the whole building, with the relationship between the stones. In the Craft's concept of the individual Mason as a building stone cut from the quarry, the First and Second Degrees are concerned with personal development while the business of the Third Degree transcends personal considerations. The second idea centres around 'designs'. Heretofore, the Apprentice and the Craftsman have been working to criteria which have been established for them, but the designer has substantially more freedom of action to determine the form of the structure he will bring into being. This notion of vastly increased scope of action is communicated directly by the configuration of the Great Lights in the Third Degree. The Compasses (representing the Spirit) are no longer constrained by the Square (representing the Psyche) as they have been in previous Degrees, and the person who has reached this level of consciousness is said to be 'at liberty' to use the capabilities which the Compasses represent; to 'render the Circle of his Masonic duties complete'; to operate consciously in (or in contact with) all Four Worlds.

If the Tracing Board and Great Lights give an indication of vastly increased scope for the Master Mason, the Ornaments of a Master Mason's Lodge give an insight into the frame of reference within which he operates. The Porch is the entrance to the Holy of Holies, the place in the Temple of Solomon where the Shekinah, the manifestation of Divinity, was said to be present. In the traditional cathedral architecture, this place is represented by the Tabernacle where the Blessed Sacrament, the Body of Christ, is reserved. Within the individual, it is the place where the Divine Spark resides. Thus, the person with the consciousness of a Master Mason operates at a level in contact with Divinity, and his consciousness is illuminated by Divine Light, which enters through the dormer window (in the roof) of the Porch. The Square Pavement has reference to the Physical World (the fourth World, traditionally represented by a quadrilateral figure), and the fact that he walks on it reminds us of the fact that he is to be a conscious bridge between all the worlds. Here we hark back to an admonition which the newly raised Master received long ago, 'without neglecting the ordinary duties of your station in life' – no matter how far the Masonic journey takes him.

The environment of a Master Mason's consciousness may seem awesome, but the consideration of the tools which are given to him to accomplish his work will cause us to realise how desperately important it is that he should have direct access to Divine guidance and how serious are the consequences if he should ignore it. As with the Tools of the previous degrees, the Master Mason's Tools are three – one active, the Pencil; one constraining, the Skirret; and one mediating, the Compasses. Note that while the Apprentice has tools of labour (action), the Craftsman, tools of testing (morality) the Master has tools of design (creativity). These tools, like all the others, are functions of the psyche; but they are so far removed from ordinary consciousness and experience that it is impossible to speak of them except by analogy, and then only briefly.

When one writes, physically, with a pencil, a unique event takes place. At the point of the pencil the thought in the mind of the writer 'changes worlds' from its place in the psyche to appear as written words on the physical paper. In this way, there is, at the pencil point, an interface, so to speak, between the World of Forms and the World of Making. This phenomenon is a direct analogy of an event which occurs deep within the psyche at the point symbolised by the Pencil. It is an interface between the Spirit and the Psyche, between the World of Creation and the World of Forms; and it is consciously available to, and under the control of the (real) Master Mason. Even when working from the customary level of ego consciousness we can, on occasion, catch a glimpse of the operation of the Pencil. The best description of the experience might be 'revelation'. It may be only a new perspective, or it may be an insight into some principle which we had not recognised previously, or it may be a realisation which shatters our existing concepts of reality; but whatever its scale, the quality of the Pencil's operation is that it causes us to gasp as we realise that the revelation is entirely new and that it has come in a flash – 'out of the blue'. That is literally the case, since the Pencil is a tool which introduces substance from the World of Spirit.

The Skirret is a tool used to mark out locations on the ground. Its string, connected to the fixed pin, acts as a constraint on the Pencil which makes the mark. This tool of limitation has substantial flexibility – the length of string is variable at the will of the user; and it must be used carefully – if the string goes slack it is of no value; and if the centre pin is improperly placed, serious errors are introduced. As the psychological function which balances the Pencil's revelation, we can think of the Skirret as representing 'understanding'. In this context, understanding should convey the impression of slow, patient, steady, painstaking work which is accomplished, perhaps, over a period of years. It is work which requires not simply logic, but reason and integrity, as it seeks to comprehend fundamental laws in all their aspects. The completion of this work comes not with the gasp of revelation, but with a whispered sigh as we say, 'Ah – at last, I understand.'

These ordinary notions of revelation and understanding are mere shadows of these psychological functions as they are available to the Master Mason who is expected to use them with facility in his minute-by-minute activity. It is extremely difficult to give examples of these tools in practical use, but we might get the barest feeling for the process by considering the work of Isaac Newton. When he observed the apple fall in his garden, he experienced the operation of the Pencil. Falling apples had been observed for tens of thousands of years, but Newton recognised, in a flash of insight, that all objects attract one another by their very nature. It was an entirely new thought – out of the blue. Several years later he published the *Principia* – the Skirret which contained his insight and gave it form. It explained the event, related it to other phenomena in a coherent fashion, and established the direction of scientific thought for the next two centuries. That is the real scope and capacity of the Working Tools of a Master Mason.

The example of Newton illustrates the balance which is required between Pencil and Skirret. Without the labour and understanding which produced the *Principia*, the revelation of mutual attraction would have remained an interesting flash of insight. Without the revelation itself, the *Principia* would not have been possible. The balance between the active and passive psychological functions at the level of intellect is achieved by a conscious capacity represented by the Compasses. As used in the Craft, the instrument is not Compasses at all, but Dividers which are used to establish proportion. They embody, in the two legs of a single instrument, the active and passive principles which run throughout the entire psyche (indeed, throughout the relative universe) and which are at last integrated at the hinge which joins the two legs. At this point of joining the Compasses of a properly functioning Human Being are in conscious contact with Divinity; and this contact enables the Master Mason to balance and control the creative and constraining psychological functions throughout his psyche and body.

It goes without saying that one who has actually been given these working tools has to exercise the greatest care and discretion in their use. For this reason one must have controlled his physical nature, squared and tested his moral and psychological functions, and died to that concept of himself which would use these tools for his own purposes before he is permitted conscious access to the psychological functions which the tools represent. That is why real Master Masons, the people of any tradition who have real knowledge of themselves, are usually modest and retiring – frequently to the point of self-effacement.

Two cautions need to be given about these Working Tools and the capability they imply. First, one should not shrink from the task, saying that Creation is the province of Deity. It is true that Creation is the province of Deity but there is no intention here to usurp that Divine prerogative. The human capacity to create is the inevitable consequence of the fact that mankind is made 'in the image of God'. The task of the Master Mason (which is the ultimate role of every human being) is to surrender his will to that of the Deity, and to stand in King Solomon's Porch, in the Divine Light from the dormer window, with his feet on the Square Pavement, and be a bridge across the Four Worlds. And he must do it consciously and of his own free will. Second, one should resist the temptation to think that one can 'put off' the use of a Master Mason's tools until he has achieved a more elevated consciousness. Remember that the tools are functions of the psyche, and they operate continuously (albeit unconsciously) in every human being. The question is not whether to use the tools, but rather whether or not to use them consciously and in the service of the Deity.

The (real) Master Mason labours in a place and at a task which is hardly known to the ordinary world. It is usually a lonely job, but he has the ability to call for help, when he requires it, upon a body of human beings called the Sons of the Widow. This group take their name from the Physical World, the 'Mother Earth', cut off, that is, widowed, from the Divine connection by the event we have described as the Fall. In other traditions these people have been called, 'The Blessed Company of Saints' or the 'House of Israel'. The Craftsman comes from the west, seeking instruction, the Master Mason, a Son of the Widow, comes from the east, seeking that which was lost. They are travelling the dimension of consciousness and the goal is to repair the loss. For that reason, the Master Mason provides instruction to his less experienced Brethren.

CHAPTER 6
The Way of the Craftsman

1 THE LODGE AS A WORKING GROUP

Throughout this book we have been considering the Lodge in its capacity as a model of the psyche. In this last section we will touch briefly upon the other principal (but infrequently observed) aspect of the Lodge; a group of people working to apply the principles of the Craft to their own experience and to realise in their own consciousness the levels of awareness symbolised by the Degrees. These considerations of practical work must be brief, because this aspect of the Craft is intensely personal; but we can outline some general principles which, if carefully observed, will lead the serious Apprentice to a situation in which he can undertake more formal work.

Generally speaking, one does not undertake interior work alone. In the broadest sense the traditional form of study in the western world is a group which meets periodically to contemplate some body of text or scripture. Each member of the group in turn reads a paragraph, after which the members discuss the implications of the text, analyse the principles it contains and (if possible) give examples of the operation of those principles in their own experience. This sharing of experience and perspective among the members of the group provides each with a richer insight into the text and to its application to his own life than he might otherwise have had. In a similar way, the recognition of the principles working in another's life assists one to see them operating in himself. On occasion, this process can cause substantial emotional distress; for example, one might see one's behaviour in a new perspective and realise suddenly that he has hurt a great many people in the past. In such situations, membership in the group is a source of real emotional support during the period of crisis. The text which the group studies serves two purposes. First, it provides the context and subject matter for the discussions; and second, it provides a link through a particular school, line and tradition to the 'teaching', which is the property of the race of man. If the group is fortunate, it will have a tutor who will be able to draw out the contributions of the individual members and enrich the discussions with perspectives which would not otherwise be available. Such a tutor is usually only one step ahead of the other members. He may be attracted to a group or one of the members may develop into the role. In either case, the position of the tutor is one of extraordinary responsibility because the other members of the group will have placed the guidance of their interior development in his hands, and he is in a position to do them real psychological damage. The role of tutor of a working group requires the greatest personal integrity; and as a general rule of thumb, it may safely be said that the desire for the position is an automatic disqualification.

A group working along the lines outlined above is following the Way of Contemplation; that is, it is using the analytical faculty as a means to come to grips with the teaching. While this is quite a common approach in the west because it fits the western temperament and it requires very little more in the way of equipment than the text itself, it is by no means the only way of study. A group which meets regularly for prayer and meditation is following the Way of Devotion, and this, too, is a common approach which can be practised with great simplicity. The third gate to the temple, the Gate of Good Works, is the Way of Action, and is the approach taken by groups which use ritual as their means of practising their tradition. Clearly, the Masonic Lodge makes use of all three of these methods, with perhaps a little emphasis on ritual.

If one sets aside the social congenialities which ordinarily surround a meeting of a Lodge, the potential parallel between the Lodge and the traditional working group is quite clear. The ritual (on which we will touch in the next section) provides a powerful, dramatic representation of the dynamics of the individual psyche and spirit, the Lectures and Tracing Boards provide a rich field for the practice of contemplation, and the prayers provide an excellent starting point for devotional practice. This balanced combination of action, contemplation and devotion appears to have been the original concept of formal Masonic Labour and any Lodge or Masonic study group which undertakes such a curriculum seriously will find itself amply rewarded. The Craft's Ritual, Lectures and symbolic structure provide the material which directs the contemplation and provides the link to the Tradition. It is for this reason that the Craft consistently refers its student to the Volume of Sacred Law (the one of his choice) and thus to the Deity. In this sense, the Warrant of the Lodge, properly displayed at every meeting, assumes deeper importance, as does the insistence of the Grand Lodge on the regularity of contact between Masons, particularly overseas. This rigorous attitude does not only prevent Masons from becoming innocently involved with those who would seek to use the privacy of the Craft improperly for their own purposes. It also defines the line through which the Craft traces its connection to the root teaching; it is a matter of fundamental importance.

The Worshipful Master of a Masonic Lodge functions in the same way as the tutor of a working group. The serious nature of the tutor's responsibilities are reflected both in the obligations of the Second and Third Degree and particularly in the prerequisites for the position of Master of the Lodge, which are outlined early in the Ceremony of Installation. To some extent, he should be able to 'provide light and instruction to the Brethren of [his] Lodge' according to the 'genuine principles of the institution'. To accomplish that he requires some real spiritual contact himself and to the extent of that connection he is entitled to the 'Worshipful' style. All the cautions mentioned above in connection with a group tutor apply with additional emphasis to the Worshipful Master of a Lodge which proposes to participate in the serious work of the Craft. This is because the honours and deference which form an important part of the ritual's symbolism can have a distinctly detrimental effect on the Master's ego.

In the usual course of events, very few Masons give their attention to the Lodge in its capacity as a working group. Such Lodges are rare at the present time. There are some, however, and to visit one is a worthwhile experience. To be a member of one is a real privilege. At the present time, as fewer candidates present themselves, Lodge calenders become, consequently less crowded. Lodges thus relieved of their heavy schedule of ritual have the opportunity to reflect on this interior aspect of the institution which they perpetuate.

2 INDIVIDUAL LABOUR

It may be that the reader will find that these ideas are meaningful to him, he may feel that there seems to be something to this interpretation and that it may be worth pursuing. The question then arises, 'What do I do next?'

Should such a one not be a Mason, he should realise there are many idioms by which this work can be undertaken, and that of these the

Craft is only one. A person interested in this work should take some care in evaluating a group or school before joining it. We have indicated the importance of integrity on the part of those who teach in this work. Sadly, some tutors fall short of the mark, and they should be avoided. In general one should be wary of any group which solicits membership. A very useful rule for evaluating any working group is that it should be hard to find, harder to enter and easy to leave. If it does not meet these criteria, the group is probably better left alone. Should one be convinced that the Craft's idiom is appropriate for him, he must petition a Lodge for the Three Degrees, because it is not possible to practise the Craft properly outside the framework of a Masonic Lodge. Such a person must be prepared to do a substantial amount of independent work because the point of view expressed in this book is not widely found in the contemporary Craft. None the less, Providence has a way of directing serious seekers, and the door of a Masonic Lodge is certainly a way into the Mysteries.

It is more difficult to give advice about individual practice to one who is already a Mason and who wishes to pursue the Craft from this point of view. The ideas that follow provide only the most elementary outline, but they too, if seriously practised, will result in providential direction, which in the last analysis is the only kind worth having. One of the most important considerations is an appropriate attitude toward authoritative statements (including those in the preceding pages), and the best attitude one can adopt is 'sceptical faith'. We can learn a great deal from the student of physics in a contemporary university. He reads about a principle in his text book, then he attends a lecture on the subject, finally he goes to the laboratory where he conducts an experiment which demonstrates the principle. The faculty of the university is trying to encourage the student in the use of the scientific method, which avoids faith in authority and relies entirely on data collected in controlled experiments. But the circumstances surrounding the educational process poses a dilemma because, if the student does not 'believe' the authoritative material in the text and lectures, he will have to recapitulate the entire history of science in the laboratory in a single year. In practice, the student does 'accept the authority' of his tutors, trusting that the science faculty will not mislead him, but he verifies their teachings with his own work in the laboratory. A student wishing to practice the Craft in the way we have considered it should adopt a similar point of view. He should receive the guidance of his teachers with tentative acceptance, but he should verify his teachers' statements in his own experience. And like the physics student connecting wires for an experiment in high voltage electricity, the student of interior work should not undertake work he does not understand or which violates his common sense.

As far as practical work is concerned, first, learn the Ritual. The plain labour of learning it by rote is an exercise which will limber up those psychological functions symbolised by the Gavel (repetitive action) and the Chisel (communication). Then participate in the ritual whenever possible. Ritual is a peculiar thing. Badly done, it is worse than useless; but ritual which is well done is, in itself, not enough. The essential point is that to perform complicated ritual properly one must be awake; and being awake makes one receptive to the meaning which is implicit in the ritual and symbols.

Second, make use of the Opening and Closing. We have seen that the Lodge is a model of the individual psyche which shows the person to have, at his centre, a contact with Divinity. The Ceremonies of Opening and Closing the Lodge represent the opening of the consciousness to that Divine Centre and closing it again with reverence. A brief analysis of the Opening will be of assistance to those who would use it in this way. The ceremony starts when the Master knocks, in response to which the Tyler presents himself and is posted. A similar process posts the Inner Guard. This fragment of ritual symbolises the process by which one makes one's self secure from interruption and turns one's ego consciousness from the concerns of the physical world to the Temple within (symbolised by the Lodge). With the Temple secure, the Master names each Officer and reviews his duties. From the perspective we have adopted, we can understand this part of the ritual as recalling and activating each level of consciousness in the psyche in turn. Before declaring the Lodge open, the Master invokes the blessing of Deity. This piece of ritual, which takes only a moment, is of critical importance. No one should undertake interior work without Divine permission; and if, for some reason, that permission is withheld, the work should be postponed – the Lodge should not be opened. Only after the assurance of the approbation of Deity does the Master open his Lodge and commence the labour of the evening.

In order to use this ceremony in one's own work, one should set aside a period each day for devotion and meditation; open that period by reciting the Ceremony of Opening, make such prayers, devotions and meditations as one's conscience and religion direct, and close the period with the Ceremony of Closing.

Third, familiarise yourself with the Lectures and with the material to which they refer. It will give an insight into the philosophical turn of mind held by the early practitioners of the Craft. Learn to draw the Tracing Board of each Degree. Practice until you can draw them from memory. As you draw them, review in your mind the principles which are represented by the various objects as they are discussed in the Lectures. The Craft's symbolism is internally consistent. Remember the rule that the symbolic structure cannot be changed; refine your concepts of the symbols until they reflect the consistency which is inherent in the Craft. Remember that the principles are operating within you and in the world every day. Observe their operation and understand what is happening to you.

Lastly, remember your Lodge at regular intervals. This is a very old practice among groups involved in the work, and has various benefits. For the individual, the process of remembering is, again, an exercise of the Gavel and Chisel. For the group, it is much more. A group (or Lodge), like everything else in the relative universe, exists in the several worlds. By calling the Lodge into consciousness and thinking about it, one invests psychological energy in it, and it becomes 'sharper' at the psychological level. There are a few Lodges whose members have practised this remembrance diligently for many years, and entering such a Lodge is an unforgettable experience. Visitors sense the 'atmosphere' and never fail to comment on it. Although they do not understand it, they know it is different, welcoming, dedicated. One who wishes to use this practice should call his Lodge and Brethren into his consciousness daily at regular intervals, say 10.00 a.m., Noon and 3.00 p.m.; recall the obligations they have to each other and the world, and commit them to the Deity with a brief prayer, perhaps the Tyler's Toast. The process should not require more than thirty seconds.

These exercises of individual labour are all that can, or need, be given in such a book as this. If they are practised faithfully, they will produce tangible results of great benefit. But one who would walk in the Way of the Craftsman must do one thing more. He must remember, always, that he is building a temple to God. He is building an edifice in consciousness in which he, himself, is an individual stone. In time, each human being will square his stone and place it in that temple, and when that temple is complete, God will behold God in the Mirror of Existence and there will be then, as there was at the beginning, only God.

To all poor and distressed Masons
   wherever dispersed over the face
   of Earth and Water;

Wishing them a speedy relief from
   all their suffering and a safe
   return to their native country;

Should they so desire it.

Note for American Readers

In England in the latter half of the eighteenth century there were two bodies which claimed jurisdiction over the activities of Masons in that country. (In fact there were four, of which only two are of real significance. For a complete treatment of the subject of early history of the Grand Lodge of England see: John Hamill, *The Craft* (Crucible, 1986) and Harry Sadler, *Masonic Facts and Fictions* (Aquarian Press, 1985)). These two Grand Lodges, generally referred to as the 'Ancients' and the 'Moderns', enjoyed a lively, and sometimes tempestuous, competition; and it was inevitable that this rivalry should be reflected in the North American colonies. In the decades prior to the American Revolution there was general agreement among the American colonists that the English government was not treating them fairly. There was, however, substantial disagreement about the remedies which were appropriate. While many thought that independence was the only satisfactory solution, there were also numerous people who felt a strong allegiance to the Crown and were disinclined to break that connection. While it would be overstating the situation to say that Masonry in the colonies was divided on this issue, it is true that the Ancients, who were generally the more egalitarian of the two bodies, tended to attract members who were inclined toward independence, while those who felt a strong connection with England often found their way into Lodges chartered by the Moderns. At the end of the Revolutionary War this pattern of membership resulted in a marked reduction in the influence of the Moderns over Masonry in the United States. As Grand Lodges formed in each of the States they did so largely from Lodges which originally owed allegiance to the Ancient Grand Lodge; and those Modern Lodges which remained were, in general, assimilated into this system. As a result, the symbolic structure which is characteristic of American Masonry was derived, generally speaking, from that of the Ancient Grand Lodge (and also from Scottish Lodges).

The situation was quite different in England. Both Grand Lodges were well established, and by the beginning of the nineteenth century it was clear to many members of both bodies that it was in their best interests, and the best interests of Masons generally, that the Craft be governed by a single authoritative body. To accomplish this a Lodge of Reconciliation was formed by an action of the two bodies which merged to form the United Grand Lodge of England in 1813. The task of the Lodge of Reconciliation was to formulate the symbolic structure and ritual which was to be used by the United Grand Lodge. In doing so, it used material from both Modern and Ancient workings and this produced a symbolic structure which, while containing some new material, is in many ways more representative of general Masonic practice and thought than either of its progenitors. It is this symbolic structure which is interpreted in this book. However, an American Mason will find that the symbolic structure devised by the Lodge of Reconciliation differs in some ways from that used in the United States, since the American symbolism did not pass through that evolutionary process. With this in mind we will comment briefly on the differences between the two systems and on how the American Mason might interpret the symbolism with which he is familiar in the context set out in this book. (The material presented in this book is by no means a comprehensive treatment of English Masonic symbols. For such an examination see: Colin Dyer, *Symbolism in Craft Freemasonry* (A. Lewis, 1976)).

The basic structure of the English and American craft symbolism is very similar, in general terms, and only two areas of difference require our attention here. These are the Officers of the Lodge and the Working Tools. In the American jurisdictions one finds that a Private Lodge has six officers; a Master, two Wardens, two Deacons, and a Tyler. To these, Lodges formed under the English constitution add a seventh officer, the Inner Guard. He is stationed inside the Lodge, at the door; and he controls access in and out under the direction of the Junior Warden. When we consider the Lodge as a model of the human psyche (which is one of the principal notions upon which this book is based) we will attach considerable importance to the Inner Guard, who performs a role comparable to that of the ego. In interpreting the American symbolic structure, we must conceive that the Tyler incorporates the functions of the ego/Inner Guard into his own office. This is not an unreasonable interpretation, since it places the ego outside the Lodge, on this side of the threshold of consciousness, which is symbolised by the door of the Lodge. This is, of course, the situation which is commonly found.

With respect to Working Tools, English Lodges recognise three tools belonging to each Degree; and in this book we will consider one of each set to be active or expansive, another passive or containing, and the third co-ordinating. In the American jurisdictions the Apprentice has only two tools, the Gavel and the Twenty-four-inch Gauge. In interpreting the American tools we should say that the Gavel represents force, passion and active psychological functions, while the Gauge represents mental processes, analysis, and the containing functions, and that it is the business of the Apprentice to keep them in balance. We can be encouraged in this view by the fact that Albert Pike advances a similar notion in *Morals and Dogma*. The tools of the Second Degree are identical in both systems and do not require our attention in this note. The English tools of the Third Degree, and the concepts they represent, do not appear to be alluded to directly in the American symbolic structure. None the less, the tool which is identified with the Master Mason in American Lodges is, like those considered in these pages, concerned with the relationship between stones. Thus, although the emphasis is different in each system, the symbols in both systems indicate that the work of a Master Mason transcends individual considerations and relates to a trans-personal activity.

These brief comparisons of English and American Craft symbolism will, it is to be hoped, present sufficient stimulating clues to enable the American Masonic reader to relate his own symbolic structure to the ideas which are presented in these pages.

Index